THE HERALD DIARY

Ken Smith

BLACK & WHITE PUBLISHING

First published 2009
by Black & White Publishing Ltd
29 Ocean Drive, Edinburgh EH6 6JL

1 3 5 7 9 10 8 6 4 2   09 10 11 12 13

ISBN: 978 1 84502 274 7

Typeset by Ellipsis Books Ltd, Glasgow
Printed and bound by MPG Books Ltd, Bodmin

Contents

Introduction vii

1 Relationships 1

2 Pearls Before Swine 9

3 Celebrities 17

4 Airdrie's Curious Car 25

5 Religion 33

6 Obituary 39

7 Restaurants 45

8 Snow White and the Six Dwarfs 51

9 Bunion Barbie 63

10 Teething on a Jet Plane 73

11 The Law 83

12 Holidays 91

13 Getting Back on Your Feet 99

14 Sport 105

15 Women Who Lunch 115

16 Pub 121

17 Barking Mad 131

18 Second to None 135

19 Worth a Study 141

20 Daughter's day 147

21 Three Yards of a Start 155

22 Taking Your Teeth Out 163

23 Sell By Date 169

24 Shopping Around 173

25 Our Lovely Politicians 181

Introduction

Every day Scots go out armed with their dry wit and black humour. Whatever the occasion they can rise to the challenge of a deadpan yet funny reply.

Fortunately when many such occasions occur, they then let *The Herald* newspaper's Diary column know about it, making The Diary one of the most popular newspaper columns in Scotland.

Here are the best gems mined from The Diary in recent years with thanks to readers for a great selection of pictures.

1
Relationships

RELATIONSHIPS are always a difficult area for the average Scotsman, who finds difficulty in expressing his emotions. As one Scots folk singer once said at a concert: "My next song is about a Scotsman who loved his wife so much he almost told her."
Here are some others who also came close.

JOHN Grant in Cumbernauld hears a chap in the pub moan: "I thought I was being funny when I told the wife how I was looking forward to her birthday next month as I had never made love to a 40-year-old. "She brought me back down to earth when she pointed out that I hadn't made love to a 39-year-old either."

A CHAP in a Merchant City bar on a Friday night asked a young lady if she would like a drink. "No, thanks," she told him. "I'm waiting for my second wind."

"What?" he replied. "You've got a Red Indian boyfriend?"

SITTING in the sun outside a west end bar, we hear a female tell her pal that perhaps her friend's new boyfriend was a tad on the diminutive side. However, her friend was taking no criticism.

"He may be four foot six," she replied, "but if he stood on his wallet he'd be six foot four."

A CLYDEBANK reader says he was a neutral observer when his wife and his 20-something daughter, who still lives at home, began bickering about the young lady being overly picky about boyfriends.

He felt he had to say something, though, when the discussion got so heated that his wife declared: "It's just daft to think you can wait around for the perfect Mr Right.

"I didn't."

WE THOUGHT the chap was being particularly louche in the pub the other night when he was discussing the hot weather with an attractive blonde. When she said she fancied a car with a sun roof, he told her with a straight face: "Yes, it would give you a bit more leg room."

JIM Fitzpatrick tells us about the Glasgow chap who goes downstairs for breakfast to be met by his wife at the cooker who tells him: "You've got to make love to me this very moment."

Thinking it's his lucky day, he accedes to her request, only to ask afterwards: "What was that all about?"

"The egg timer's broken," she tells him.

NIGEL Manuel in New York tells us of a Wall Street banker pal lamenting the market collapse and telling him it was even worse than a divorce. "I've lost half my net worth," he explained, "but I've still got the wife."

A CHAP who was supposed to be taking his girlfriend out on Saturday night got into bad company at the pub, lost all track of time and turned up at his girlfriend's flat two hours late.

By this time she had assumed he wasn't coming, stormed to her room, took off her outfit, wiped off her make-up, threw on a dressing gown and was sitting at the telly in a foul mood eating Jaffa cakes.

On reflection, he told his mates, he shouldn't have looked at her and said: "Two hours late – and you're still not ready to go out."

A STUDENT working evenings in a Glasgow call centre tells us that when he asked one caller about her marital status, she replied: "I guess we're as happy as any couple these days."

ONE of the Scottish soldiers returning from a tour of duty in Afghanistan tells us one of his mates was getting such a slagging when they were abroad by putting up a picture of his much-cared-for Peugeot hatchback with alloy wheels while all the rest of the squad sported pictures of their girlfriends.

The car chap eventually snapped back: "Laugh if you want – at least my car will still be there when I get back."

"As he comes from Milton, that was a pretty big boast," says our contact.

"MY WIFE's the double of Kate Moss," said the loud-mouth in the bar the other night.

"Kate's eight stone, and my wife's sixteen stone."

"I GAVE my wife a ring for our anniversary," said the loudmouth in the bar. "I said, 'Happy anniversary, I'm finishing early today so have my tea ready for five.'"

JOHN Hutchison in Hertfordshire tells us: "A chap comes home and finds his wife in bed with his best friend.

"'Tommy, how could you?' he says. 'I've got to, but you?'"

"THEY'VE started a support group," said the loudmouth in the bar the other day, "for women who can't stop talking."

After a pause, he adds: "It's called On and On Anon."

DO WE believe the tale of the married couple out for dinner when the wife asked why her husband kept on looking over at the woman in the drunken stupor at the next table?

"It's my ex-wife," replied the husband. "She's been drinking like that since I left seven years ago."

"Unbelievable," replied his new spouse. "I wouldn't think anybody could celebrate that long."

AND DO WE believe the reader who claims he overheard a woman in a bar tell her female pals that she and her husband usually ended up in the doggie position in bed. While her friends stared at her she then added:

"Yes, hubby sits up and begs. And I roll over and play dead."

WE ARE told that a Whitecraigs lady went in to her local newsagents to pay for her newspapers being delivered and explained that as she had recently become divorced, she was reverting to her maiden name.

"Is the address still the same?" asked the assistant.

"Yes," replied the customer.

"Still, you managed to keep the house then?" replied the assistant.

READER Frank Eardley tells us about a Celtic fan, eagerly awaiting an expected championship win that season, telling his mates about being in the Celtic shop the day before the final game of the season.

"You know how fate sometimes intervenes in your life?" he was saying.

"I was in the Celtic shop and they were selling personalised mugs, and in front of me was one with my wife Karen's name on it.

"Of course, I had to buy it, combining the things I love most in life. "Coffee and Celtic."

WE HEAR of a North Sea oil worker who had calculated that he would be offshore on his silver wedding anniversary, but, rather impressively for a Scottish chap, he arranged for his local garage to deliver a silver £9,000 Corsa car to his wife on the big day.

When he arrived onshore, he was congratulating himself on his thoughtfulness as his wife showered him with kisses until she said: "Very extravagant for our 24th wedding anniversary."

He now has a whole year to work out how he is supposed to top that next year.

A READER spots an advertisement for a powerful Suzuki motorbike which is for sale with only a thousand miles on the clock. The advertiser states: "I'm selling it because it was purchased without proper consent of a loving wife. Apparently 'do whatever you want' doesn't mean what I thought."

READER Jim Corr was reading an advertisement for bedroom furniture which stated: "Excellent condition canopy bed. One night stand and a bench seat also included," and he thinks to himself: "That's quite an offer, but I don't think my wife would approve."

"MY WIFE wanted me to take her somewhere expensive on Friday night," declared the chap in the pub. "So I took her to the BP garage."

A WOMAN at a drinks reception tapped a chap on his shoulder and said: "Hello." When he turned round, she looked puzzled, and blurted out: "Oh, sorry. You're not the man I thought you were."

"My wife says that all the time," he told her.

2
Pearls Before Swine

MORE from the battleground of the sexes, where alas drink is often used as the social lubricant that slips down too easily.

TOM Tumilty tells us of the research which claimed that Scottish men spend more time on foreplay than men from any of the other home countries.

When Scottish husbands smugly pointed out this finding to their wives, they were told that 30 minutes of whining, begging and pleading did not constitute foreplay.

THE WOMAN having an after-shopping spritzer with her pal in All Bar One in Glasgow was discussing her wedding plans, and whether she should have something meaningful engraved on the inside of her future husband's wedding ring.

"How about 'Put it back on,'" suggested her pal.

AH, THE BITTERNESS of the west of Scotland male. A chap in the pub asked his mate if he still played games with his wife.

"Yes," he replied. "We play this game where we sit making sarcastic remarks at each other until one of us finally cracks and leaves home. Been playing it for years, but no-one's won it yet."

A WOMAN in Glasgow's west end was telling her pal about the benefits of going to see a therapist. "It's great," she said. "You spend an hour just talking about yourself. I suppose it must be like being a bloke going out on a first date."

WE OVERHEAR a chap in the bar tell his mates: "I'm always falling out with the girlfriend. I told her that in the six months we'd been together we hadn't agreed on one thing.

"'Seven months,' she replied."

DAVID Stevenson avers he was reading *The Herald* in an Edinburgh coffee shop where the headline "UK patient is first to be pregnant by pioneering technique" was spotted by a Morningside matron at the next table who muttered to her friend: "With the lights on?"

WE WATCHED in a Glasgow wine bar as an emboldened chap went up to two women having a glass of wine, pointed at the neck of one of the women, and asked: "Are these real pearls?"

Not that keen on being interrupted, she gave him a curt: "They are."

But he ploughed on anyway with his rubbish patter and said: "I could bite them with my teeth to see if they are real."

The poor sap gave up, however, when she snapped back: "No, I think your teeth would also have to be real to do that."

A GROUP of Newton Mearns husbands were discussing how much their wives used their joint credit cards, with wild claims of excessive spending. One told his pals: "My wife actually took something back to get a refund on the credit card. The bank immediately phoned and said there had been unusual activity on the card they wanted to check."

A NEWTON Mearns reader tells us her husband was off work for a bank holiday and offered to help around the house. But when she was in the bathroom having a shower, he knocked on the door to ask her what should he feed the kids for lunch.

PICKWICKS TAVERN
HUSBAND CRECHE
DOES HE ANNOY YOU ON THE BEACH?
GET UNDER YOUR FEET AS YOU SHOP?
WHY NOT LEAVE HIM HERE
AND PICK HIM UP LATER?
NO CHARGE, JUST BUY HIS DRINKS

Upset with the interruption, she shouted out: "Just do what you would do if I wasn't here!"

She came out of the bathroom to hear her mobile phone ringing, and when she answered it, on the line was hubby from downstairs asking: "What should I feed the kids for lunch?"

"I THINK my girlfriend had 61 boyfriends before me," said the loudmouth in the bar the other day.

"At least, I think that's what she means when she calls me her sixty-second lover."

DRIVING in heavy M8 traffic, Stephen Murray, of Glasgow, found himself admiring the legend freshly etched by a finger-tip on a filth-spattered lorry's tailgate: "A dog is for life – not just for Saturday night."

ONCE AGAIN we notice how brave men get when they gather for a pint. We hear one chap in a Glasgow hostelry who declared: "The wife was complaining about her car being too old and said she wanted something that went from nought to 80 in four seconds.

So I suggested the bathroom scales."

TWO LADIES waiting for their flight at Glasgow airport are in the cafe where the cleaner clearing the tables admired the make-up bag they had on the table in front of them. Seeing her interest, they told her where she could buy a similar one. But as she pushed her trolley with the empty plates to the next table, she told them: "I don't need to bother with anything like that hen – I've got a man."

WHO says Scots can't express their emotions? Andrew McAllister was working in a pub on Arran when a regular was asked how he felt about the imminent arrival of his partner's baby. "Not 'excitit' excitit," he explained.

"Mare the excitit yous get when yer up in court."

A GROUP of lads in a Glasgow bar were giving advice to one of their number who was getting married. "When listening to your favourite CD," said one, "turn the volume up to where you want it, then turn it down three notches – it will save your wife from coming over and doing it."

WE OVERHEAR one wife in discussion about her husband coming back from an office do uproariously drunk. "What did you do?" asked her pal.

"Well, I confronted him with a three-pronged attack," she declared, then added: "I jabbed him in the arm with a fork."

A GLASGOW reader was trying to console her husband who, despite having a fear of dentistry, was having to go that day for some root canal treatment.

"I'm only going to visit my mother," she told him. "If I could swop places with you, I would."

"No, you're all right," he foolishly replied. "At least I'll get an anaesthetic where I'm going."

THOMAS Law meets a woman called Norah Knight and thinks he may have worked out why she never had a boyfriend from Glasgow.

EVEN on the bitter-cold nights of February, Glasgow girls are still wearing tight, revealing outfits. But it was unfair of the chap in Yates's Wine Lodge, who commented to his pal about a passing lady: "She looks like she's been poured into her clothes . . . but forgot to say 'when.'"

"WOMEN . . . so hard to please," said the chap in the east end boozer at the weekend. "Valentine's night, booked a table for me and the missus for eight o'clock," he told his pal.

"But her face was still tripping her. I swear it was half eight before she'd even potted her first red."

WE OVERHEAR a chap in a west end wine bar telling a female customer at the bar that women often compared him to Brad Pitt.

As she turned to return to her pals' table with a bottle of rioja, she merely told him: "I can imagine they do compare you. Do they tell you he's good looking and you're no'?"

"FELL OUT with the girlfriend," said the chap enjoying a Fair Friday pint with his mates.

"She said she wanted to discuss our future.

"I said it would be exciting, with personal rocket ships to transport us around the world, and bionic limbs if we ever lost one.

"But apparently that's not what she was talking about."

"THE WIFE was complaining," said the chap in the pub, "that I never listen to her.

"Or something like that."

3
Celebrities

SCOTS have a curious relationship with so-called celebrities. They enjoy meeting them, but rarely let them get too big-headed about it. Many a travelling Scotland fan in the Tartan Army has gone up to a celeb and asked if they can have a picture taken. When the celeb simperingly says yes, the fan hands the celeb the camera and poses in front of him with his mate.

FORMER president Bill Clinton had a round of golf at Prestwick before a speaking engagement at a plush charity event in Glasgow. Local caddy Buff, who carried Clinton's bag, was asked if he had called him "Bill" or "Mr President".

"Ah, well, all the way round the course," said Buff, "it was Bill. But when he gave me a $200 tip at the end, then it was Mr President."

SWEDISH actress Britt Ekland, at the Edinburgh Fringe to do a show talking about herself, swished in to the Assembly Rooms' club bar with her chihuahua, Tequila, which goes everywhere with her, tucked inside her handbag.

Dogs are generally not allowed in the club bar, so staff pretended they couldn't see the tiny chihuahua "poking its head out of the bag like a meerkat," as one of them put it, with Britt constantly muttering: "Down, Tequila, down."

It all ended badly when Britt dropped her bag and watched helplessly as the dog rolled out on to the floor.

"She can't hold her Tequila," as one onlooker murmured.

RETIRED All Blacks captain Sean Fitzpatrick, capped more than 90 times for New Zealand, was explaining the fickleness of fame to the audience at the Scottish Marketing Excellence Awards.

In his taxi to Heathrow Airport to come up for the awards, Sean realised that the driver was eyeing him closely in his mirror until finally blurting out: "Give us a clue."

So Sean modestly replied: "I used to play for the All Blacks."

"No," replied the taxi driver. "I meant: international or domestic departures."

FORMER drug-raddled popster Pete Doherty described a visit to Dundee as his biggest regret.

Not the city itself, we should point out, but his decision to stage-dive – throw himself off stage into the arms of adoring fans – at a gig there.

Says Pete: "This big Scotsman just grabbed hold of my pants and said, 'Cop a load of this, Doherty!'

"When they found me on the bus I was crying my eyes out going, 'The band's not working out. I think we should split up,' "Nobody believed that was what's wrong, and eventually I snapped, 'All right! I got a wedgie, OK?'"

CHART-TOPPING singer-songwriter James Morrison began his latest tour playing to a sell-out crowd in Glasgow's O2 Academy. During his show, he told the audience that he had a special affinity with Glasgow as his nan came from the city.

"She used to give me bags of sweets and tell me, 'Go on then, rot your teeth, you wee b*****d,'" he happily recalled. Yes, you can't beat the warmth of a Glasgow granny.

THE RECENT honorary degree awarded to veteran crooner Engelbert Humperdinck by Leicester University reminded Michael Gartlan of a visit to Glasgow some years ago by The Hump, who experienced the unique Glasgow ability of putting folk in their place.

Engelbert was brought into a quiet bar by a journalist interviewing him, and the singer began handing out autographed photos which had, it must be admitted, been taken some years earlier, judging by the youthful mien.

One regular accepted the signed picture with a "Thanks very much Mr Engelbert", looked at it then added: "That yer boy is it?"

IRVINE Burns Club has unveiled its latest exhibit – murals by the late Edward Odling of Burns which were rescued from the renovation of the Burns Heritage Centre in Alloway.

A director at Irvine recalls when earlier Odling murals of Burns were displayed at the club's museum in the sixties, and were visited by actor John Cairney, who has made the study of Burns his life's work.

John noticed that the topcoat worn by Burns in the Odling paintings was hanging in the museum and, clearly believing that the coat was a genuine Burns relic, he tried it on.

Overcome with emotion, he declared: "I can feel the spirit and blood of the Bard coursing through my veins."

No-one had the heart to tell him it was an old army blanket fashioned into a coat to help the artist finish his painting.

THE GUSHING tributes to the Queen on her 80th birthday remind Dave Kemp in Inverness of an Inverness Courier article many years ago describing the Queen performing the official opening of Raigmore Hospital. Cheerily describing the desperation of patients trying to see the monarch, the Courier stated: "Patients peered from their beds, and those lucky enough to be in wheelchairs blocked the entrances to all the wards."

READER Andy Moffat from Rutherglen was at the Bob Dylan concert in Glasgow when not all fans appreciated, he tells us, the fact that Bob sang a lot of his newer material rather than just playing safe by trotting out his greatest hits. Finally, one exasperated fan shouted: "Hey, Jimmy! Do you know any Bob Dylan songs?"

GLASGOW's former Lord Provost Liz Cameron, presenting the Freedom of the City to businessman Lord Macfarlane, explained that a member of Lord Macfarlane's family was at the hairdresser before the grand occasion, and when asked by the stylist, in time-honoured tradi-tion, if she was going somewhere nice, explained: "It's a special occasion. A member of my family is getting the freedom of the city."

"That's nice," replied the hairdresser, who then ventured: "How long was he in for?"

TOP-SELLING author Alexander McCall Smith whose fame origi-nally came from his Botswana-based *The No 1 Ladies' Detective Agency*, is aware that the occasional critic claims that not enough happens in his gently paced books. He dismisses such criticism by cheerfully arguing: "There's enough happening in the world without authors adding to it."

FORMER Yes keyboard player Rick Wakeman, at the Edinburgh Book Festival to talk about his biography, *Grumpy Old Rockstar*, recalled a booksigning where a fan informed him that he'd signed a pair of her knickers 20 years ago, and then politely asked him whether he would mind doing so again, for old times' sake.

Rick was slightly taken aback when, instead of simply taking a pair out of her bag, she asked that he sign while she was wearing them.

As he did so he heard a more elderly lady further down the queue mutter to her pal: "Oh Flora, I do hope we don't have to do that."

SINGER David Essex is still touring, and appeared recently in Glasgow where an adoring middle-aged fan handed him a bracelet which glows in the dark. David was struggling to clip it on, so another concerned fan rushed up and motioned for him to hold his wrist down so that she could help.

As she worked away, he looked down and asked: "You're not trying to steal my watch are you?"

GLASTONBURY Festival, that grand-daddy of all outdoor music festivals, included Auchtermuchty legends, The Proclaimers. When Proclaimer Charlie was asked whether he would invite strangers into his back garden to drink excessively, play loud music and piddle recklessly, like Glastonbury Festival founder Michael Eavis does, he replied: "It's a bit like that when my wife's family come to visit from Glasgow, to be honest."

AND the famous Proclaimer twins, Craig and Charlie Reid, told their audience in Glasgow the other day that they were still bemused by one question they were asked when doing a series of interviews in America. "How did you two meet?" the earnest interviewer asked them.

SCOTS singing legend Lulu, was the surprise guest at the Tulloch Group Christmas party in Aviemore, when she cheerily turned to one of the lady guests, and told her: "I love your shoes – whose are they?"

She was perhaps not expecting the rather abrupt reply: "Mine."

PUBLIC relations guru Russell Kyle once explained what happened when comedian Billy Connolly met the then Celtic owner, Fergus McCann for the first time. It was a title-winning game and they were taken for hospitality in the Celtic boardroom, but at the last minute Russell realised that Billy was wearing a smart T-shirt, and not the regulation collar and tie expected on such an occasion.

As Fergus was a stickler for such rules, Russell whispered to Billy that something might be said about his attire. But as Fergus bore down on Billy, the Big Yin shouted: "Fergus, how are you? Lovely to meet you, but what kind of football club are you running here? I took my tie off two seconds ago and some bastard's gone off with it!"

SINGER Midge Ure, who received an honorary degree in Dundee from Abertay University, also opened the uni's student centre where he unveiled a commemorative plaque made from recycled CDs.

Midge told them that if only they had contacted BMG Records about unsold copies of his solo albums, the plaque could have been much, much bigger.

RADIO Scotland presenter Fred MacAulay was recalling when he walked the Great Wall of China to raise money for charity, and while there, remembered that Scotland was playing in an important football tie. Working out it was now midnight back home, he thought the best option to get the result was to phone BBC security, which he did, explaining he was at the Great Wall of China, and asking for the Scotland score.

He then heard the security guy say to his mate: "I've got Fred MacAulay on, pissed in some Chinese restaurant."

KEITH Allen, actor and father of singer Lily, tells of being in The George in Wardour Street with Scots actor Robbie Coltrane, who was in a tartan suit with fluorescent pink socks and red brothel-creepers.

Bemoaning the pressures of fame, as he often does, Robbie wailed: "Ah can't get down the street without bein' bothered."

Replied Keith: "I hate to be a killjoy, Robbie, obvious as it is that you are wallowing in the most enjoyable mud-bath of self-pity, but if you didn't go about in a suit that's louder than Iron Maiden, you might have a better chance of being ignored by the great unwashed."

"DID YOU see that Gordon Ramsay was getting criticised in a newspaper for some of his food at his posh restaurants being prepared elsewhere, then delivered by van?" asked the chap at the golf club bar. "He quickly reassured diners that the van had four Michelin tyres."

4
Airdrie's Curious Car

Not all the humour, of course, comes from Glasgow. Here is a quick tour around the country.

THE BBC's Gaza correspondent, Alan Johnston, who spent four months as a hostage, was guest speaker at Dollar Academy's annual dinner in Edinburgh. After a moving speech, Alan inquired if there were questions from the audience, and was asked: "You spent some time in Dundee – was that a good preparation for being held hostage in Gaza?"

SHAME on the reader who tells us that part of Airdrie town centre was sealed off after a suspicious item was spotted in a car. It later turned out to be a tax disc.

GLASGOW writer Colin MacFarlane tells of the disorientation many Glaswegians felt when they were moved to the new council housing schemes.

The story was told, says Colin, of the wee woman who had lived in a tenement all her life who was moved to the 20th floor of a multi-storey flat. She went missing shortly afterwards, the police were told, and they searched all her old haunts but with no sign of her.

Three days later she was found on the ground floor of the multi-storey clutching a scrubbing brush.

When police asked where she'd been, she replied: "Somebody told me it wis ma turn tae dae the stairs."

A WEBSITE offering houses for sale in Scotland hurriedly removed the advertisement for a modern flat in Glasgow's south side which declared it was in "the thieving area of Gorbals".

It returned later rewritten as thriving.

VINTAGE TV journalist Alan Whicker revealed how, as a gauche 19-year-old second lieutenant, he was overjoyed by news of his first promoted posting. "When I looked at the letter telling me where I was to meet up with the Devonshire Regiment, I thought 'Whicker's luck! They're sending me to somewhere in the South Seas ... an exotic hula-hula kind of a place – how marvellous.'"

Soon afterwards, Alan found himself billeted in Alloa.

ACTOR John Cairney tells of a well-known English actor who was in Glasgow to record an episode of the television series *This Man Craig*. He told John that he'd been asked to speak at a dinner, but didn't feel his plummy Home Counties accent had gone down particularly well.

When he asked the audience if they could hear him at the back, a Glasgow chap shouted out: "Perfectly well. But I'm happy to change places with someone who can't."

JOHN also recalls the story about the legendary Chic Murray being woken by a knock at the door of his Glasgow flat. When he opened it, he was asked if Chic Murray was at home. Chic, in his poshest drawl, informed the caller that "Mr Murray is not at home, but would you care to wait in the library?" The visitor's face beamed, but as he stepped forward Chic put out a hand and continued: "Fine. If you go back downstairs and turn left at the close, you'll find it on the corner of the next street. A lovely big sandstone building. You can't miss it." Then closed the door.

COMEDIAN Jimmy Carr, appearing in Òran Mór in Glasgow's west end as part of the Glasgow Comedy Festival, said how impressed he was with the regeneration of Glasgow, saying of the west end: "Well done on this bit – it looks just like Edinburgh."

And referring to Mothers' Day he asked if there were any mothers in the audience. "Proper ones," he explained. "Not just those who have done it for a council flat."

AN ANONYMOUS and very cheeky Paisley reader alleges that following the recent publication of statistics pertaining to benefit payments, Glasgow is now known in government circles as Incapa City.

COMEDIAN Frankie Boyle offered his services for free to an Amnesty International gig in Edinburgh where he explained to the visitors to the capital in the audience that they hadn't seen the real Scotland until they had been to Bathgate.

"I was once on a bus going through Bathgate at night and I saw a man urinating against a front door – then he opened the door and went in."

REMEMBER the Monty Python sketch about the Yorkshire millionaires claiming they once lived in shoe boxes at side of motorway? It came to mind when we read the website of Inverclyde housing association, River Clyde Homes, which held an exhibition on social housing at Greenock's Oak Mall.

One exhibition visitor wrote: "I remember me and my brothers would be waiting for my dad to come back from work on a Friday.

"Not that he would give us money or anything. It was the rubber band on his pay packet we would fight over.

"The hours of fun you would have with that rubber band if you were lucky enough to get it."

Ah, happy days.

WE PASS on from the internet a number of ways in which you can tell that you're Scottish:

- Scattered showers with outbreaks of sunshine and a cold northerly wind are your idea of good weather.
- You only enjoy *Weir's Way* on the telly, late at night, when you've been drinking.
- You are able to recognise regional dialect, such as Glasgow's "Orrite pal, gauny gies a wee swatcha yir paper'n'at, cheers, magic pal" or, from Aberdeen: "Fitlike, loon? Furryboots ya bin up tae? Fair few quines in the night, min."
- You are unsurprised to find one shop selling all of the following: pizzas, nappies, cigarettes, curries, milk, paint and shoes.
- Scotland go 2-0 up against the French, and you immediately think that getting beat 3-2 would be "no' a bad result".
- You have been to a church wedding where the football results have been announced during the service.

THE PRINCESS ROYAL was helicoptered in to Wishaw General before opening the £2m headquarters of diamond drilling and concrete cutters CVD Group at the Eurocentral industrial park off the M8. A member of her entourage was asked if they could not have landed somewhere a bit closer. They replied that they had originally planned to land at a park in Uddingston, but added that they had been informed that the helicopter was unlikely to be there on their return.

A READER driving through Crook of Devon up Clackmannanshire way noticed on one of the road signs below "Crook of Devon" someone had neatly written "Twinned with the Thief of Baghdad".

WE HEAR of a radio phone-in where the question was: "Name the UK's second city."

A chap from Birmingham phoned in and declared: "I think it's Birmingham – we're second biggest, after all."

This was followed by a chap from Edinburgh who stated: "I think it's Edinburgh – we are a capital city, you know."

Finally, a Glaswegian phoned who asked: "Any chance it's London?"

WEST enders parochial? Surely not. It's just that we hear of a chap from Glasgow's West End on a business trip to Beijing, China, who texted his mates to say that he would not be out in the Chip Bar as usual on Friday night as he was "in the Far East".

His mate texted back: "Dennistoun?"

"DID YOU see the zombie film, *Outpost*, was filmed in Govan?" said the chap in the pub the other night.

"No problem getting extras, then," replied his mate.

5
Religion

Religion has always been intertwined with Scottish humour. These are some of the tales.

WE HEAR from a teacher in a Catholic school in Lanarkshire who told her first-year class, during a discussion about Jesus, that he had, in fact, been born Jewish.

This astonishing piece of information was absorbed by the class in stunned silence until a hand went up. "Miss," said the questioner, "when did he convert?"

SEEN on the notice board of a church in Greenock. "If the last time you were in church a big man called you names and threw water over you . . . it's time to try again."

WE OVERHEAR a chap moaning to his mate about how miserable his brother was, and how he was grumpy all Christmas, and how he bought cheap and nasty presents for his nephews and nieces.

He then ended with the line: "In fact, I think the only reason I keep in touch with him is in case I ever need a kidney or bone marrow."

KILMARNOCK Round Tablers wheeled Santa around town all week on the back of a truck to entertain the town's young folk.

When Santa asked one wee girl if she was excited about Christmas, she told him: "A'm so excited I ate my whole advent calendar in one day."

MARTIN Patience, an Eaglesham lad who foolishly became interested in journalism during a work placement on The Diary, is now a BBC foreign correspondent, and once in Jerusalem wanted to investigate the phenomenon known as The Jerusalem Syndrome, where some foreign tourists find the Holy Land experience so intense that they believe they have become biblical characters.

Having heard that a Swedish man, who thought he was Jesus, was staying at a local hostel, Martin asked at reception for him, only to be told he had left the previous day.

However, seeing Martin's disappointment, the receptionist tried to help by adding: "But John the Baptist just booked in this morning."

"I GET fed up," said the loudmouth in the bar the other night, "with people becoming celebrities simply because they've got famous parents."

"What," replied his pal, "like Jesus?"

A YOUNGSTER got home from guising on Hallowe'en and complained to his folks that every house slammed the door in his face.

"Told you you shouldn't have gone as a Jehovah's Witness," said his dad.

TWO work colleagues, returning to the office after a boozy Christmas lunch, both commented that the drink must have been really strong as they both had blurred vision. Later in the afternoon they realised they had picked up each other's spectacles by mistake.

THE SEASONAL nativity plays remind Annette Christie of her west-end church taking youngsters to perform at a centre for the homeless in Glasgow. As they trooped into the centre, one worthy standing outside drawing on a roll-up asked: "Whit's goin' on in there the night, hen?"

Annette told him: "The children from our church are doing their nativity play."

He took a further drag before asking: "Oh, aye. Whit's it aboot?"

FED UP with cutesy Christmas stories? Well what about the chap who told us: "I got out the Christmas decorations and among them I found a present for the kids which I'd forgotten to give them last year. Imagine how excited they were.

"Pity it was a puppy."

THE CHRISTMAS season reminds one Ayrshire teacher of when she explained the story of Baby Jesus being born in the stable because there was no room at the inn. She avers that after the Christmas break one of the little ones in her class asked her: "See those folk you were talking aboot. Have they got a hoose yet?"

THE CONGREGATION of Dumbarton Free Church arrived one Sunday to find a "To Let" sign on the lamppost outside the main door to the kirk. They were relieved, however, to discover it referred to a flat across the road. Someone, though, in the congregation has a sense of humour. By the evening service the sign had been altered to read "Pews To Let: Apply Within".

READER Gerry McCulloch spotted three chaps on Hallowe'en dressed as the colourfully clad oddities Dipsy, Laa-Laa and Po from the *Teletubbies* taking some time to persuade a doorman in Glasgow's Royal Exchange Square to allow them ingress.

Just as they were eventually allowed in, the purple-clad fourth Teletubby, Tinky Winky, waddled up after being delayed at a cash machine. Stopped at the door, he argued that his pals had just been allowed in.

The bouncer, in total seriousness, shouted at the other three chaps in yellow, green and red costumes who had gone ahead:
"Hey, is this guy with you?"

ON HALLOWE'EN, a trendy young thing from Glasgow went to work in Larbert in a beautiful vintage 1950s white dress with polka dots, plus red cowboy boots, which she had bought on holiday in America. Going for a drink with colleagues afterwards, she was surprised when the pub manager handed her a bottle of champagne at the end of the night.

Unbeknownst to her, she had won the bar's Hallowe'en costume prize as Alice in Wonderland.

THE EDINBURGH businessman at his office Christmas party was just a little bit too loud as he announced that his wife had just bought "a Glasgow Christmas tree".

When his colleagues looked a bit puzzled he brayed: "It leaves needles everywhere."

A DUNOON reader standing in for Santa at a local housing group tried to dampen one lad's expectations of getting the Power Ranger toy he asked for by saying that they were so popular, his elves in his workshop might run out of them.

The young lad told Santa that if he was stuck he should go on to eBay where there were hundreds for sale.

THE ARMISTICE service reminded reader Ron Parr of an aunt who had never been in the countryside in her life until she joined the Land Army at the start of the Second World War and was sent to Golspie to help on a farm.

The first job was milking, and the farmer, in the interests of hygiene, wanted the udders cleaned first, so told her to "go and wash the beasts before they get milked".

He subsequently went in to the milking parlour to find a row of bemused cows all with shiny clean faces.

THE LAUNCH of The Official History of Celtic Football Club, and the key role played by former owner Fergus McCann, reminded reader Kate Wilson of when Fergus married retired Church of Scotland minister Effie Campbell's daughter.

Effie talked to a Church of Scotland Young Women's Group meeting at the time to describe her family's reaction to the news.

"We've never had a Catholic in the family before," said one family member. "Yes, but we've never had a millionaire either," replied Effie.

WE ARE TOLD that, when one of Glasgow's gangsters was killed, his brother said to the local priest that he would donate £5,000 to the church if he would say at the funeral that his brother had been a saint.

It gave the priest quite a dilemma. So at the funeral he told the mourners that the dead man had indeed led a life of womanising, thieving and violence.

He then added: "Mind you, compared to his brother he was a saint."

6
Obituary

If there is humour in religion, then humour in death is never far away.

A GOUROCK reader back from a cruise to the Canaries tells us that, sadly, there were a couple of deaths on board owing to the elderly nature of many of the holidaymakers. Rumours on board had spread, however, that the death toll was even higher, so when our Gourock chap found himself sitting next to the ship's doctor for dinner that night, he asked if the rumours were true. "When you get ice cream for breakfast," the doc told him, "you'll know the fridge is full."

KEEN environmentalists who want to ensure the most biodegradable form of a funeral can now order caskets made from basketweave material. Reader Frank Eardley saw a hearse going past the other day in Edinburgh with one such coffin and heard a chap beside him declare: "I can't make my mind up if that's a funeral or a very dull picnic."

LEADING Scots entertainer Christian, was signed up by ground-breaking Paisley funeral directors J & W Goudie to tour nursing homes with Goudie staff, performing, and bringing some festive cheer in the run-up to Christmas.

Locals refer to the tour, good-naturedly, as "Goudie's annual stock-take".

THE DEATH of blues singer and songwriter John Martyn, who grew up in Glasgow, reminds us of John telling the tale of American singer Rosemary Clooney appearing at Glasgow's Pavilion Theatre on a Saturday night when the crowd was a bit boisterous.

So noisy were the audience that Rosemary's attempts to begin failed because of the racket, and the crowd didn't shut up until someone at the back of the hall bawled out: "Haw! Let the old bag sing!"

In a second, the Pavilion fell quiet and Rosemary announced: "Thank you. I'm glad that there is at least one gentleman in the audience tonight."

A HIGHLIGHT of the Fizzers exhibition – caricatures of famous Scots – at the National Portrait Gallery was the long-faced cartoon of comedian Rikki Fulton, drawn by artist Tommy Sommerville shortly after Rikki had been diagnosed with Alzheimer's.

When Tommy returned to Rikki's home a few weeks later with the completed drawing, Rikki's face lit up as he exclaimed: "That's fantastic!"

Rikki then turned away, his face fell and he asked: "Who is it?"

After a few seconds of excruciating silence as Tommy wondered what to say, Rikki winked, telling him: "Ah, you thought it was the Auld Timer's kicking in there."

A WOMAN of a certain age attending the Blast From The Past charity concert, which included the Glitter Band and Alvin Stardust, was surprised when a T Rex line-up took to the stage with a rather chunky bloke with curly hair doing a passable vocal impersonation of Marc Bolan. "Blimey," she told her pal, "Marc didn't hit a tree, he hit a pie shop."

HOW DO police officers deal with the sad task of informing relatives of a loved one's death? Russell Martin tells us he raised this very issue when chatting to policemen. One experienced officer insisted it was no problem. "We're specially-trained to handle delicate situations," he declared, alleging that he once visited the bereaved McTavish household, removing his cap before treading softly to the door. He continued: "I then eased open the letter box and shouted, 'Is the widow McTavish in?'"

TWO WOMEN were studying the *What's On* programme for the Glasgow Royal Concert Hall when one of them pointed out that Gordon Smith, the psychic barber, was coming to the hall in April, and that he was famed for his powers as a medium.

"Not for me," her friend declared crisply. "My mother gave me a hard enough time when she was alive – I'm not giving her another chance."

THE MEMORIAL service for broadcaster Clement Freud reminded a reader of when Clement stood for the post of Rector at St Andrews University, and some opponents questioned whether he was too old.

Clement replied at a hustings meeting: "A great deal has been made of the fact that I'm 78. Don't worry, as this is an entirely temporary situation. "Next year I fully intend to be 79."

TV PRESENTER and raconteur Gyles Brandreth tells the tale of the last time he appeared on telly show *Countdown*. He went into the dressing room of the late, lamented Richard Whiteley who told him there was a hole in the wall through which you could see into co-presenter Carol Vorderman's dressing room.

After a dramatic pause for effect, Richard then added: "I was going to call maintenance and get it mended, but then I thought, 'What the hell? Let her look."

THE HERALD'S obituary on ebullient advocate and sheriff Rosaleen Morrison described her as one of the funniest women comic Billy Connolly had ever met.

This was confirmed by one of her legal brethren who tells us that when Rosaleen was a magistrate in Hong Kong, the local newspaper once phoned her to comment on local solicitors complaining that they found it distracting when she appeared on the bench wearing see-through blouses without a bra. Rosie replied that she couldn't see what the problem was, and would only be concerned if the complaint had been that they could see her breasts through her tights.

7
Restaurants

Nor is food far from the thoughts of the average Scot.

DUNCAN Macleod tells us about his seaman brother who ordered a giant lobster claw in a Rio de Janeiro restaurant. Unfortunately the claw was in a scabby condition, badly cracked and chipped. When he complained, the waiter told him it was due to the lobsters fighting in the tanks.

"Well" replied Duncan's brother, "take this one back tae the kitchen and bring us oot the winner."

A READER tells us about asking a waitress for tomato ketchup. She returned with a tiny container with just about enough to dip one chip in. Our reader merely raised it to his mouth, pretended to take a sip, and told the waitress: "That's great! I'll take a bottle, please."

LLOYDS TSB, sponsors of the Scottish Bafta awards for film and television, gave everyone a scratch card at the after-awards dinner in the Hilton Hotel. One lady scratched and won a bottle of champagne. A waitress duly arrived with the bottle and whispered with Glasgow caution: "If you open it we'll have to charge you £25 corkage."

YOU CAN take the girl out of Cumbernauld . . . a young Lanarkshire woman in London on business was whisked to the upmarket award-winning Nobu Japanese restaurant where the helpful waiter, while she stared at the menu, asked if she was allergic to anything.

"Yes, cats," she replied, thinking of her occasional sneezing bouts.

Then, realising the waiter was still staring at her and fearing he may have misunderstood, she ploughed on, declaring: "Not that I'm suggesting you cook cats here."

Which really should have gone unsaid.

A YORKSHIRE businessman dining at the world-renowned Three Chimneys restaurant on Skye became impatient at the length of time it was taking for his food to arrive, and drew this to the attention of a waiter.

The waiter, as politely as he could, told the diner that the food would be through as soon as possible, but "quality takes time". This cut no ice with the chap, who told him with typical Yorkshire bluntness: "See outside? That's my Bentley parked there. It's quality, and it's bloody fast."

A READER hears a classic misunderstanding in his canteen at work, where a young chap sits down and asks someone further down the table for the salt, which he then liberally pours over his dish.

The person passing the salt, possibly concerned about his health, asks the chap: "Should you not taste it first?"

"Naw," he replies. "All salt tastes the same, doesn't it?"

ITALIAN rock legend Zucchero, famous throughout Italy, but less well known here, was appearing at the SECC in Glasgow in front of an audience composed largely from central Scotland's Italian community.

Five minutes after the scheduled start time, there was a hushed anticipation of the great man's appearance.

An older Italian-looking couple arrived late, and as they took their seats, the gentleman surveyed the audience and loudly exclaimed: "Jeez oh. How's anyboady in Glesga gonnae get a fish supper the night?"

A TALE from Ardrossan, where it is claimed a local worthy was looking particularly glum in the pub, and when asked what was wrong, declared that he had put on a pot of stew that morning and had nipped out for a quick pint while it was simmering.

While out, some local ne'erdo-wells in his close, he reckoned, had broken in to his house and out of pure devilment had defecated in the pot.

The shocked barman asked what he did about it.

"Well, ah hud to throw hawf it oot," he replied.

MOTHERWELL reader John Park passed a pub with a blackboard outside on which was written: "Chef's special." Someone had rubbed out the dish below it and chalked instead: "And the barman's pretty cute too."

"DID you hear about Andrew Lloyd Webber?" asked the holidaying chap in the pub. "Despite the millions he's made, he walked into a branch of Burger King and asked for a Whopper."

The toper added: "The guy behind the counter told him, 'OK, sir, your musicals are fantastic.'"

READER Chris Terris was in a coffee shop in Glasgow when he realised he had no spoon with his coffee, and went back to the front of the queue where he asked the server if he could have a stirrer.

The Glasgow chap at the front of the queue offered Chris the services of his wife.

"I SAW a notice in McDonald's," said the chap in the pub the other night, "which said they don't accept £50 notes.

"Now who, with fifty quid in their pocket, is going to eat there?"

8
Snow White and the Six Dwarfs

"NOW I know I'm getting old," said the chap in the pub the other night. "I was getting my haircut and the barber asked if I wanted anything for the weekend.

"When I said yes, he offered me his caravan at Saltcoats."

A BLUES fan tells us that, at the recent Glasgow gig of blues guitarists The Nimmo Brothers, Stevie Nimmo was performing his well-known solo where he repeats a riff ever more quietly until it is barely audible as a hush descends throughout the audience. At the climax, he hardly even plucks the strings at all.

The ambience, though, was shattered by a voice from the back enquiring: "Is the sound man awa' for a pish?"

SPEAKING at the Trades Hall dinner in Glasgow to mark the election of quantity surveyor David Dobson as the new Deacon Convener, Professor Brian Williams, president of the Royal College of Physicians,

All business transferred to
The Tanning Shop
14 Fade Street
beside the market bar
phone: 679 8929

said he had been asked to exclude in his Toast, any reference to race, gender, religion, Peter Mandelson or banking practices.

"So I will now," said Brian, "mime my Toast."

Fellow speaker Sir Kenneth Calman, Glasgow Yoonie chancellor, and chairman of the commission on Scottish devolution, said you could learn a lot about a city by understanding its humour.

"What Glasgow says today," he declared, "the rest of the world tries to pronounce tomorrow."

HAMISH MacQueen tells us about a friend who bought a house on Mull with the Gaelic name Tobar Dubh – Black Well. He was so taken with the name that he spent days digging around the extensive garden to see if he could find the original well – but, despite his backbreaking efforts, he had no luck.

He was later talking to the local shopkeeper, who told him about the previous occupants, then added: "Before them there was an English couple, the Blackwells."

A DARNLEY reader was creosoting his garden hut at the weekend while being watched by his neighbour. As he stepped back to admire his handiwork, he remarked: "I didn't expect it to come out that colour."

His neighbour told him: "Aye, Ah had a girlfriend who came out the tanning salon that colour. She wasnae happy either."

A RENFREWSHIRE reader was a bit upset when she went into her laundry room and discovered a dead fieldmouse in her washing machine.

Her mood wasn't helped by hubby looking round the door and surmising: "Oh, well, at least he died in Comfort."

"WHEN Madonna first moved to England," said the loudmouth in the bar the other night, "she said she wanted to feel more English.

"She is now an unmarried single mother with three kids from different fathers.

"Job done!"

BOB Bain, who helped organise the exhibition on the history of the Glasgow pantomime at Kelvingrove Art Gallery, reminds us of the classic tale of *Snow White* at Glasgow Pavilion when at the last minute one of the diminutive actors playing one of the seven dwarfs went off sick.

Without a replacement, the director changed the script so that there were only ever six on stage at any time with lines like shouting off stage: "Grumpy, you stay there and guard the castle."

At the finale the six would take the curtain call and when they seemingly noticed there was one missing, one would go off and look for him, then quickly change costume and come back on as the missing dwarf.

OUR STORY of the barmaid supergluing the sleeping customer's tie to the bar reminds Des McDougall in Lenzie of when he was a young

subaltern in the Indian Army, and a major from another unit spent a night at their mess.

Says Des: "He turned out to be an arrogant loudmouth, got very drunk and passed out in an armchair. I and another subaltern got a hammer and nails, took off his shoes, nailed them to the floor, and replaced his feet. About five in the morning people were rudely awakened by horrendous yelling as the major awoke, tried to move and convinced himself he was paralysed."

A GLASGOW businessman tells us he noticed his personal assistant study her horoscope every morning in the newspaper, and eventually he said to her: "I always thought you were too levelheaded to believe in astrology."

"Of course I don't," she told him.

"Don't you know how sceptical we Capricorns are?"

INEBRIATION in Glasgow's city centre of a weekend evening is not a pretty sight. Nevertheless a Diary reader did smile when he saw two youths emerge from the Subway at Buchanan Street on Saturday night with one opining: "Ah don't know whose house that was, but that's some train-set he's got in his cellar."

A DRIVER visiting Glasgow for the first time noticed on the overhead gantry on the M8 motorway at the city's boundary the flashing sign "Keep your distance", and he thinks to himself: "Whatever happened to Glasgow's legendary friendliness?"

READER Alan Kelly is also bemused by the overhead gantry signs on motorways. "I read the sign 'Check Your Tyres', so I stopped and gave them a good warning."

AND BARONESS Barker remembers when she was driving her mum on the M74 and the gantry sign stated: "Remember to fasten your seat belt".

Her mum declared: "Isn't that nice. They've looked into somebody's car and seen that he's not doing it. It's good of them to put him right."

READER BILLY Stewart argues: "I'm always disappointed when I see a sign saying 'Mud on road'.

"It's news of a Showaddywaddy comeback tour that I'm waiting for."

STORIES about disappointing DVDs remind Jimmy Manson in Ayr: "My pal bought the video *Three In A Bed*. There was some disappointment when he found it was the life story of darts champion Jocky Wilson."

A BISHOPBRIGGS hubby took the dangerous move of pointing out to his wife that the exercise bike in the living room – that she had she bought in the sales – was now gathering dust and what was the point of it?

She calmly pointed out that she gets extra exercise having to walk round it every evening and morning to close and open the curtains.

IT TOOK him a while, but a reader eventually understood the mobile call he overheard in Glasgow's Buchanan Street where a young woman was angrily telling someone: "When I say I'm going to call, and I don't call, I just don't see why you can't call to see why I didn't call."

A BBC4 programme *It's Time to Go Nationwide*, which celebrates the old teatime telly magazine programme *Nationwide*, reminds Glasgow-based former BBC man John Thompson of when he worked on the show in the early 1980s.

A film of a skateboarding duck was big hit on the programme, so the hunt was on to find other unusual ducks. When a farmer in Norfolk phoned to say he had the oldest duck in Britain, a film crew rushed to his farm, only, says John, to career into the farmyard, drive straight over the aforementioned duck and flatten it.

NOT all *Nationwide's* stories were about farm animals, of course. John recalls when a crew went out to film a religious cult which based its beliefs on those of native North Americans.

Their views, although sounding slightly odd in Britain, were being treated sensitively by the *Nationwide* team – until they were about to start filming and one of the crew snapped down the clapperboard and shouted: "Nutters. Take one."

It took hours, says John, for the cult to be talked back into giving the interview, and a new clapperboard operator was found.

THE *SEX AND THE CITY* film, loved by its female audience, does not, of course, reflect life here in Scotland.

This was brought home to one reader watching the movie about the glitzy glamour of New York at the Quay cinema in Glasgow. He saw a woman in front, halfway through the viewing, hunker down in her seat, fish out her mobile phone, and whisper into it: "Did you remember to switch off the soup?"

THE FATALISM of Glaswegians was laid bare by former Lord Provost Liz Cameron at the opening of the splendidly refurbished City Halls and Old Fruitmarket in the Candleriggs. She explained that the council's architects were working on the site when they pulled down a cheap

Formica wall in the old bar area and found behind it a magnificent Victorian rehearsal room that no-one knew was there. Delighted with their find, they rushed round to the LP's office, burst in and told her: "Lord Provost, we've found something in the Halls!" Liz looked up and wearily asked: "Oh my god. Asbestos?"

A READER tells us about an office night out at a comedy club where quite a reserved chap made the mistake of going to the loo during the main turn, and was verbally lacerated from the stage. The heat from his face, apparently, could have powered a three-bar fire.

Our reader was then amazed when another chap stood up and walked to the loo, only to be bawled at by the turn: "Where are you going?"

But in a Glasgow accent he gruffly replied: "I'm going for a pee before the comedian comes on," which left a deafening silence from the stage.

POKER is, of course, growing in popularity, so much so that a number of pubs are running poker nights. At one such night in Glasgow recently a chap picked up his two cards and announced: "A pair of kings."

He then looked at the faces of the other players staring at him, and slowly added: "I said that out loud, didn't I?"

ARCHITECT Bob Menzies was telephoning a firm in the English capital for a catalogue where the sarf London receptionist asked for his name. After carefully spelling out his surname, which can be somewhat tricky to some folk, he then added: "R for Robert."

The catalogue arrived addressed to Mr Arfur Robert Menzies.

A READER tells us he overheard two girls talking at the taxi rank outside Central Station in Glasgow. One told her pal: "You're really on the game, you are."

Fearing a conversation about the girl's morals, he was relieved to hear her reply, after a moment's thought: "I think you mean 'on the ball', ya eejit."

ROY Hay in Australia tells us of a local club where members were taking part in a charity parachute jump. As part of their training, the instructor was telling them to prepare themselves for landing once they were about 90 metres from the ground.

"How do you know you are at 90 metres?" asked one woman.

"A good question," replied the instructor. "At 90 metres you can recognise the faces of people on the ground."

The woman thought about this for a while before asking: "What happens if there's no-one there you know?"

9
Bunion Barbie

KEITH Murray tells us about a relative working for ScottishPower who asked a caller for his postcode. That is, after all, usually enough to identify where the caller lives. This time, though, the postcode did not show up on the computer, so she then asked: "Do you have a street name?"

"Aye, well ma pals call me 'The Iceman' sometimes," he replied.

OUR story about the confused ScottishPower customer reminded Marie Murray of the customer who walked into the ScottishPower showroom where she worked to tell them he had taken over the tenancy of a house.

Seeking proof of the changeover, she asked: "Have you got your missive with you?"

"Naw," he replied, "she's up in the hoose."

OUR story about the computer spellchecker coming up with Jesus being betrayed for 30 pieces of liver, reminds BBC Scotland's home and social affairs correspondent, Reevel Alderson, that before computers, copytakers at news organisations were creating similar faux pas. His favourite was the story about a grey seal cull. The BBC copytaker typed that the Secretary of State for Scotland had given the go-ahead for a Gracie Fields cull on Orkney.

A FEMALE reader tells us she had volunteered to do face-painting for the weans at her church's fund-raiser. Before she started, she popped into the church hall's loo to paint her own face clown-white, with added purple eyeshadow and garish red lips to advertise what she was doing.

As she finished at the mirror, another woman leaving the loo touched her gently on the shoulder, whispered: "Too much!" and walked past.

A CHAP taking an early-morning constitutional through his local cemetery saw a fellow walker, and shouted out a cheery "Morning!"
But the fellow he saw shouted back: "No. Just walking my dog."

"WHAT'S your favourite beer?" a market researcher asked a chap in Sauchiehall Street.
"Oh, probably the fifth one," he replied.

READER Martin Harris felt his education at Glasgow's St Aloysius'College had been in vain when he was stuck with the crossword clue"Drunk"with the missing letters _I_HT. All he could think of was the Glasgow term "Pisht". Next day he discovered it was, of course, "Tight".

WE ARE told about a young girl in Aberdeen queuing to get into a club when the steward on the door asked: "Have you got any ID?"
"About what?" she asked.

AN EDINBURGH reader was leaving his home when he noticed the girl in the flat opposite open her front door while still talking on her house cordless phone.
He was about to tell her that such phones don't work far from

the base unit when she stopped outside her open door and rang her frontdoor bell.

His mystification was cleared up when he then heard her say on the phone: "I'll have to go, mum. That's someone at the front door."

BEHAVIOUR is deteriorating at the cinema these days. A reader tells us two women who were chatting away in front of him were still talking when the film started, and he was forced to lean forward, tap one on the shoulder and tell her: "Excuse me, I can't hear."

"I should hope not," she snapped back. "It's a private conversation."

SIMON Lord in New Zealand tells us there is a professional rugby league player in Australia named Matt Hilder, who plays for the Newcastle Knights. Inevitably, his nickname is Waltzing.

THE CROWDS at the *Antiques Roadshow* filming at Edinburgh's Hopetoun House reminds a reader of when the BBC show appeared in Glasgow, and a local went along with a large metal box and told the expert: "It's been in the loft for over 60 years, we reckon, so we thought it must be some kind of family heirloom."

"Is your house insured?" asked the expert.

"Why? Do you think we should?" the Glaswegian asked.

"Probably. Because that's your hot water boiler," replied the expert.

A READER spots a vending machine on which a sign had been stuck stating:

"Diet Coke not working." Below someone had scrawled: "Try exercise then."

SPOTTED on the toilet wall in the council's building services offices in Springburn, a printed sign stating "Please Use The Toilet Brush Provided." Someone with a felt-tip pen has added: "No thanks, I'll just keep to the toilet paper."

WRITING from Prestwick, Charlie Taylor shares what may be an ancient Ayrshire wisdom – either that, or an unwarranted slur on the inhabitants of Renfrewshire's couthiest township. As Charlie insists: "If you look in the dictionary at words containing the sequence of letters "rrh," they invariably have nasty connotations: catarrh, gonorrhoea, diarrhoea and Barrhead."

WE OVERHEAR a young woman in the Outback bar in the city centre tell her pal that a mutual friend was desperate for a personalised number plate but couldn't afford to buy one. "So she's thinking of changing her name to SB04JYZ."

JUNE Elder admits that living in England for a few years has perhaps tuned out her ear to the Scottish dialect.

This was brought home to her when she was back visiting her family and attended an auction in Hamilton, where the auctioneer held up a figurine of a lady in long skirts.

Says June: "I heard the word Meissen, tapped my brother on the arm and, eyes wide with awe and suitably impressed, I said, 'Ooh, Meissen!'

"My brother, trying to stifle his mirth in the packed auction room replied, 'No, he said this is a nice yin.'"

YES, it must be an old one, but we'd never heard it before. A chap who had little luck in his love life comes across a book in a second-hand bookstore entitled *How to Hug*, thinks it might help him with his emotional issues, and buys it.

The bloke running the bookstore watches him leave and wonders why he only wanted volume eight of the encyclopaedia he had on sale.

ON the theme of mothers getting younger, Les Mathieson overheard a woman tell her pal: "I've failed as a mother. My teenage daughter has started smoking."

She then added: "Not only that, she's doing it in front of her children."

SO, DID you hear about the young lad who went home and told his parents he had bought a theatre? "Are you having me on?" declared his mum. "Well, I'll give you an audition, but I'm not promising anything," he told her.

ADVERTISING company boss John Morgan said he had recently returned to his native Govan. Being a regular Burns Supper speaker,

he popped into Govan Library to brush up on the Bard's material, and said to the librarian: "Robert Burns. The Complete Works."

"I'm sorry Mr Burns," she replied, "but the massage parlour is a bit further down the road."

"I DID some DIY with my step-ladder the other night," said the chap in the pub. "I never really got along with my real ladder."

PERHAPS it's the sunny weather that is bringing out the daft conversations, but a Glasgow reader strolling through Botanic Gardens heard a young chap say to his pal: "It's at times like this I wish I had listened to what my mother said."
"What did she say?" asked his pal.
"I've no idea," he replied. "I wasn't listening."

WITH the Barbie doll celebrating its 50th birthday, a reader assures us these are the latest models, marking the occasion:

- Hot Flush Barbie – Press Barbie's bellybutton and watch her face turn beetroot while tiny drops of perspiration appear on her forehead. Comes with hand-held fan and tiny tissues.
- Bunion Barbie – Years of disco dancing in stiletto heels have definitely taken their toll on Barbie's dainty arched feet. Soothe her sores with the pumice stone and plasters, then slip on soft terry mules.

- Mid-life Crisis Barbie – It's time to ditch Ken. Barbie needs a change, and Alonzo (her personal trainer) is just what the doctor ordered – along with Prozac.
- Post-Menopausal Barbie – This Barbie forgets where she puts things, and cries a lot. She is sick and tired of Ken sitting on the couch watching telly, clicking through the channels.
- And, of course, that old classic you will have heard about – Divorced Barbie which comes with Ken's house and Ken's car.

10
Teething On A Jet Plane

DAVID Ashford was on a tour bus to the Lakes when a husband passed a holdall to his wife and told her: "Here, haud this tae we get aff."

Unhappy with the arrangements, she snapped back: "Ah huv tae haud everything."

"No really," replied hubby. "The only thing ye don't haud is yer tongue."

A STONEHAVEN reader tells us that an oil worker who flew back to Aberdeen from outside the EU was stopped at customs for having two bottles of whisky in his luggage, and that as the allowance was for only one litre of spirits he would have to pay tax on the other.

The chap declared he wasn't paying any tax, and deliberately dropped one of the bottles, which smashed.

"That was the duty-free one," said the impassive customs officer.

ANDREW Foster of Ontario knew he was back in Glasgow when he was going through the city's airport and the metal detector went off at security.

The uniformed chap said he would have to give him "a wee pat doon" and asked what the lumpy object was in Andrew's pocket.

Andrew took out a bulging wallet and the security chap sighed: "Aye . . . ah huvnae seen one o' those since I was married," and waved him on his way.

AN ATTRACTIVE young woman arrived at Glasgow Central Station to catch the train to Manchester. Mindful that the last time she used the service it had been disrupted by line maintenance, and she had to change trains twice, she asked the chap in the smart Virgin uniform: "The Manchester train . . . do I have to change?"

"No," he told her, "what you're wearing is fine."

MUSICIAN Roy Gullane, returning from the Lorient Celtic Festival, flew in to Scotland where he was asked to step aside so that a customs official could search his suitcase. And in that chatty way they do, he asked Roy what he did for a living, while rifling his case.

"I'm a singer in a Scottish traditional folk group," said Roy, who is a member of the Tannahill Weavers.

"That's a weird way to make a living," opined the customs chap.

And Roy can't help thinking that the search may have been over a lot quicker if he had not then replied: "Not as strange as having to rummage your way through total strangers' dirty socks and drawers."

A SOUTHSIDE reader swears to us that his ageing mum was going on her first flight abroad to see relatives and was worried about the cabin pressure giving her earache. Her son told her to take chewing gum as that would help. She later told him that she took his advice, stuffed it in her ears, and it worked a treat.

A BUSINESSWOMAN flying up from London to Glasgow last week was sitting behind a mum with her two young boys. When the drinks trolley came round, one of the lads asked: "Mum, can I get a Coke?"

"No," replied the mum. "You know why you're not allowed it."

He argued back: "But I'm strapped in, Mum – I can't go hyper."

KEN Drummond in Stenhousemuir recalls the yarn about the chap buying a ticket at Larbert for Aberdeen. The clerk passed over the ticket and said: "Change at Stirling."

The chap replied: "Nae fears, I'll have ma change now."

READER David Currie was astonished when he saw an advertisement for a new Nissan gas-guzzler called the Nissan Armadale. Why would they name it after a West Lothian town? Is it an indication of how tough it is driving over discarded Buckfast bottles? And was there also a Nissan Bathgate and a Nissan Whitburn?

He realised he ought to get his eyesight checked, as closer inspection showed that it was, in fact, a Nissan Armada LE.

EX-PAT John Gerrard in Arizona tells us: "When I moved to New Orleans in 1980, I drove to the test centre with my UK licence. Being August, it was 98 degrees fahrenheit with 98 per cent humidity.

"The tester, being at least 25 stones, suggested that I go out to my car, back it out of the parking space and drive it into the one next to it while she looked out the window of the air-conditioned office.

"And so I passed."

TALES of budget airlines remind Steven Elder of the – and it must be an apocryphal tale surely – of the pilot on one such airline coming on the public address system to ask if any passenger had change of a tenner as he wanted to buy a coffee.

A GARAGE manager tells us that a customer brought in his car which had two side panels bashed in, and who told the mechanic that he was driving in the country when it was hit by "a herd of horses".

The mechanic looked puzzled and told him: "Herd of horses? Is it not a herd of cows?"

But the customer replied: "Naw, it was definitely horses."

DONALD Grant recalls flying from Leeds Bradford airport to Glasgow in a particularly rough and bumpy flight. The sweating, nervous chap sitting next to him tried to jump up as soon as the plane landed, but couldn't, and started shouting that he feared he'd had a heart attack.

A stewardess calmed the situation by undoing the petrified chap's seatbelt, which he had forgotten about.

WE ARE told about the Glaswegian who was very lucky to get through airport security when he was told he couldn't take his bottle of water through, and he replied: "Why? Is the pilot a Gremlin?"

WE ARE not that gullible, surely, but reader Paul McGivern in Paisley tells us that a bus was holding up traffic in Glasgow's Hope Street while it stopped at the lights with its hazard flashers on. The driver, in the pouring rain, was out of his cab, trying to fix his broken windscreen wipers.

A woman driver pulled up beside him, felt sorry for him in the rain, rolled down her window and asked: "Excuse me, would you like a screwdriver?" Without missing a beat, the driver replied: "Thanks for the offer, hen, but I'm running 10 minutes late as it is."

THE SMOKING ban also includes Glasgow Airport where, to cater for smokers, the airport has created smoking zones outside the terminal. To make smokers as comfortable as possible, benches have been provided, while artificial hedges have been placed around it to improve the aesthetics of the area. Airport staff have now nicknamed the area "Benches and Hedges".

A READER was queuing at the Partick Subway station in Glasgow when a noisy chap in front slapped down his money on the metal counter and barked "single" at the ticket woman. As she passed him back his ticket she sweetly told him: "Yes, but if your manners improve I'm sure you'd get a girlfriend."

ALISON Spring, in East Kilbride read a Strathclyde Buses recruitment poster on the side of a double-decker. It encouraged potential drivers to apply with the slogan: "Take on a busload of responsibility." Naturally, someone had crossed out the last word with a marker pen and substituted: "Drunks".

A READER claims that a well-dressed woman got on the train to Glasgow at Helensburgh with a youngster, obviously her grandson, and buried her face in a magazine while he looked out of the window.

After the train had trundled eastwards for a while, the little one asked: "Where are we?"

Without looking up she told him: "I don't know, Justin. But it won't be anywhere nice."

A READER on a 66 bus in Glasgow was entertained by a chap who tried to strike up a conversation with anyone who caught his eye. Eventually the chap's eyes lit on a fellow traveller wearing a stetson. So impressed was he that he leaned over and offered the stetson-wearer a drink from his bottle of Buckfast. "No thanks, I'm teetotal," he replied.

At that the Buckfast imbiber eyed him suspiciously before asking: "Ur ye whingein' or boastin'?"

A KILTED fan at Bristol Airport, heading to Paris for the memorable Scotland game (many and varied are the routes taken), eventually made it to the head of the slow-moving queue and was asked the age-old question: "Have you left your bag unattended at any time, sir?"

"Aye," he was heard to reply, "it's been in the loft for the past six months."

And not a smile was cracked.

A WORKER at an insurance office in Lanarkshire tells us they received a motoring accident claims form on which the driver had written after the question "Could either driver have done anything to avoid the accident?", the nonetheless truthful reply: "Travelled by bus?"

OUR current love of nostalgia – OK, old stories – allows us to let Stewart Smith remind us of the elderly mum from Glasgow visiting her son in America during the Glasgow Fair and being asked on arrival at United States immigration: "Ma'am, do you have any meats, fruits or any other foodstuffs with you?"

"Aw, son" she replied sympathetically. "Ah huvny even a sweetie ah can gie ye."

A BUSINESSMAN who flies frequently between Glasgow and London tells us that a woman came on board with a baby the other morning and he could see all the other business types stiffen, silently hoping that she wouldn't be sitting next to them.

Eventually, as the plane took off, their worst fears were realised when the baby began to cry.

Our businessman smiled, though, at the spirit of the baby's mother who cared not a jot, and instead sang to her little one her own version of a John Denver classic: "I'm teething, on a jet plane. Don't know when I'll not cry again."

READER Dave Biggart from Kilmacolm was flying from Copenhagen to Glasgow when he asked a steward if the pilots were Australian, which had been the case the last time he had used the service.

The Scottish steward told him in a low voice: "Naw, it's two women pilots.

"But don't worry – they don't have to reverse it."

HIRING a steam train to re-open the Alloa to Stirling rail line the other week reminded us of the old story about the trainspotting enthusiast who fell under the wheels of a steam locomotive.

He was chuffed to bits.

A READER tells the tale of the chap replacing a 6ft-long fluorescent striplight in his kitchen, and being told that the dustmen wouldn't take away the dud tube, decided to take it to work with him where it could be easily disposed in his company's large bins.

Getting on the underground, he noticed the carriage becoming increasingly busy, so he held the light up above his head. However, two other passengers who squeezed on thought it was a handrail and held on at either end.

At the next stop, the chap simply got off, leaving them with the dud striplight.

A READER was sitting beside a mother on a plane who breast-fed her baby during the flight. As they were coming in to land, the cheery steward checking seat belts, said to the mum: "He was hungry!"

"Not really," replied the mum. "It's just that my doctor said it would help alleviate the pressure in the baby's ears."

"Goodness," replied the steward. "And all these years I've been sucking sweets."

A TRAFFIC cop insists that he pulled over a very geriatric driver on the M8 who was causing a huge backlog of cars by only driving at eight miles an hour. When the cop questioned him, he said he thought the signs for M8 was the speed you had to drive at. While the officer was putting him right, he noticed that the old lady sitting next to the driver was looking a bit pale. "Are you all right?" asked the officer.

"I am now," she replied, "Now that we're off the M90."

JOANIE Madden, over in Glasgow with her Irish/American traditional folk group, Cherish the Ladies, for Celtic Connections, was recalling a flight the band took from Canada to Ireland which had to ride out a severe storm en route.

"It was so rough," she said, "that at one point I heard a commotion behind me. I turned round and about four rows back there was a man wrestling a nun for her rosary beads.

"The nun won, of course."

11
The Law

The old line is oft told – what do you call a chap in Castlemilk wearing a suit? The accused.

There is no denying though that the law can bring out the gallows humour in many a Scot.

INDEFATIGABLE advocate Donald Findlay presented the Scottish Law Awards, and it wouldn't have been Donald, of course, if he had not lobbed a scabrous joke or two at the audience. He said he once had a client who had thrown a petrol bomb into a Govan pub.

"Fortunately," said Donald, "someone drank it before it went off."

EDITH Easton tells us that a friend of her son driving to work one morning was pulled over by the police with one officer asking him if he knew why he had been stopped. When he replied no, the cop gave him a clue by asking: "What are you wearing now that you were not a little while ago?"

Completely flummoxed, and as he had just left his home, he could only stumble the reply: "Underpants?"

His face was beetroot as the officer patiently explained: "Seatbelt."

JOE Boyle from Kings Park tells us of the work colleague who claimed that the police stopped him late at night to tell him that one of his rear lights was out. Being in a bit of a foul mood, the driver got out of his car, walked to the rear, kicked it near the light, and it came back on.

The unfazed officer merely told him: "That's fine, sir. Now if you kick the windscreen will your road tax come up to date?"

A LONDON correspondent phones to tell us that the inquiry into the police actions against the demonstrators at the G20 summit has found a poster in a Metropolitan Police station looking for volunteers to work at the summit which had the headline: "Come early and beat the crowd."

DECENT, law-abiding Diary readers won't know this, but in the old days it was not unknown for scofflaws to crack the window of their electricity meters and slide a photographic negative through the gap and position it to rub against the wheel, thus slowing down or even stopping the meter.

Reader Ian Wilson was reminded of this when he met an old pal whose former house in Easterhouse was recently demolished as part of the council's latest plans to do the place up.

Ian asked if he was sorry to see the old place go, but his pal replied that the house had been nothing but bad luck to him. He had even been done for fiddling the electricity meter with a photographic negative when he lived there.

"Could you not have blamed the previous tenant?" asked Ian.

"No," his pal replied. "It was my wedding picture that they got out the meter."

A TALE from Glasgow Sheriff Court, where folk are perhaps becoming just a little bit silly over the festive period. One defence solicitor returned back upstairs to court after interviewing a client in the cells below and declared: "That's the barrel changed."

RETIRED Scottish football referee Willie Young also has a successful career as a lawyer, which is why he was saying he had to tell a client held in jail that there was good news and bad news about the analysis of some blood found at the scene of the crime.

The bad news, said Willie, was that the blood was a match for his.

"So what's the good news?" asked the client.

"Your cholesterol level is right down," said Willie.

WE HEAR about a retired police officer attending a funeral in Holytown, Lanarkshire, who was asked by a local for a lift from the church to the cemetery.

He agreed, but as the chap jumped in, the ex-cop was heard to re-mark: "Danny, I'm just thinking. This is the first time I've put you in the back of a car without a blanket over your heid."

CAN WE believe the nedette who was telling her pal: "Ah nicked a couple o' steaks oot o' Asda and the security guy came after me shout-ing, 'What are you doing with them?'

"So I shouted back, 'Tatties, peas and gravy – but what's it goat to dae wi' you?'"

A SOUTH-SIDE reader found himself a bit short of cash after a night out in the city and, somewhat disgruntled, realised he would have to

walk home. His mood was not helped when he had barely left the city centre and crossed one of the city's bridges when a pasty-faced junky stepped out in front of him and demanded money with menaces.

"Do you think I would be walking home through here if I had any money?" our reader angrily replied.

The Dick Turpin wannabe thought about this for a moment before replying: "Fair enough" and slinked back into the gloom.

A HERALD picture of actor Joe McFadden being measured for his police uniform for his role in television series *Heartbeat*, reminded Robin Veitch of when his company supplied police macintosh coats in Clydebank.

One morning a young constable came in to be measured, and

approached with his chest exaggeratedly expanded, while asking: "Is your tape long enough?" "It's OK, son," replied the chap taking the measurements. "It's your chest we're going to measure – no' your head."

A GLASGOW lawyer swears to us that he was in the sheriff court one day when the accused, giving evidence in his defence, claimed he was not there at the time of the alleged offence as he had "shot the craw".

The sheriff bestirred himself at this point, shuffled his papers, and declared: "I didn't know there were guns involved."

A POLICE officer tells us that when they investigated a chap being shot with a starting pistol, a senior officer asked if the attack had been race related.

12
Holidays

Holidays for Glaswegians of course used to be a trip doon the watter. Now all corners of the globe have the pleasure of visiting Scots.

A GLASGOW couple splashed out on an upmarket hotel in Spain where they found themselves lounging at the pool beside a history professor and his wife.

The prof turned to the Glasgow chap and asked: "Read Marx?" "Yes," he replied.

"I think it's those wicker chairs."

A READER visiting Lanark Loch noticed that the popular trampolines had a notice at the ticket booth which stated: "You must not use the trampoline if you are pregnant or you are under the influence of alcohol or drugs."

Fair enough, he thought, until he saw that the sign next to it stated that the trampolines were for under 14-year-olds.

GLASGOW's Deacon Convener of the Trades House, Malcolm Wishart, and his wife Aileen were walking across George Square after returning from an Incorporation of Gardeners outing to Benmore Gardens in Cowal. Both looked rather dapper, carrying a wicker picnic hamper they had taken with them.

But as they got halfway across the square, with the resident pigeons swirling around them, a chap with a small refreshment in him shouted out: "Haw, big man! Wan o' yer pigeons has escaped."

WE OVERHEARD a girl in Glasgow's Buchanan Galleries telling her friend she planned to buy a new mobile phone as her previous one was no longer working. When her pal asked what had happened to it, she said she'd dropped it in the sand when she was on holiday.

"And the sand stopped it working?" asked her mate.

"No," she replied. "It was fine until I took it back to my room and poured water over it to rinse the sand off."

GREAT PLACE New York. A Scots tourist taking the train from New Jersey to Penn station hears the conductor announce: "For those of you who are interested, Penn Station is next.

"For those who aren't, it still is."

A READER tells us about him and his wife visiting elderly friends, and taking with them the dreaded holiday photos.

"That's me in my sun hat and sunglasses – I was incognito that day," chirruped his wife to the couple.

"I don't know how you remember the names of all the places you've been," replied the elderly lady.

A CHAP in a Springburn bar was telling his buddies about a new suitcase he had purchased for the summer holidays which was made of the toughest material, and would handle being thrown about by even the most careless of baggage handlers.

"You could drop it off the Red Road flats," he declared, "and it still wouldn't burst open." "Aye," said his pal, "but I bet you it wouldn't still be there when you got to the bottom."

A GLASGOW couple who decided to hire a cottage in the country for the weekend proved what city slickers they were when they were walking back to the abode in the dark.

"What's that noise?" said hubby. "I thought I heard an owl."

"You probably did," replied his wife. "I just stood on the dog's paw."

SANDY McGill asked in a Glasgow bookshop if they had the book *Go Ask Alice*, which details a teenager's fight against drug abuse. He was directed to the travel section.

He can only surmise that the shop assistant assumed he had adopted the Glasgow vernacular and was asking for something called Goa's Gallus.

DO WE believe the member of the Maritime and Coastguard Agency who tells us they received a mayday over the radio stating: "Help. We're in the water!" "Capsize?" asked the coastguard.

"Medium," came the reply after a pause. "But what does that matter?"

A CHAP going to his first Burns supper anxiously asked a colleague: "What's the best thing for a hangover?"

"Drink a huge amount the night before," he was told.

A LANARKSHIRE girl on holiday in India with her boyfriend phoned her parents in great excitement the other day to say that her boyfriend had got down on one knee and proposed to her outside the Taj Mahal, arguably the most romantic building in the world.

"What a coincidence," her dad told her. "Me and your mum met outside the Pir Mahal in Hamilton."

A READER back from a cruise in America tells us that when they went ashore in Mexico they were handed a postcard of the liner which they could show to any taxi driver to take them back to the dock if their Spanish wasn't up to it and the driver didn't speak English.

So he duly flashed the card at a taxi driver, but it didn't quite work. He drove them to the post office.

A READER flying back to Scotland was at an American airport where one of the ground crew at the departure gate was speaking into her walkie-talkie, or whatever they are called these days, and telling another member of staff: "Please disregard the call for wheelchair assistance at gate A5. Repeat. No wheelchair needed at gate A5." There was the squawk of the person at the other end replying, before the crew member said wearily: "Yes, it's a miracle."

A READER was impressed when he was on holiday in Florida, and the local next to him in a pub told the barmaid: "You're in great shape. You must work out a lot."

She gave him a huge smile in return. Back in Glasgow, our reader thought he would try the same in his local where he told the barmaid: "Wow! You must work out a lot."

"You should try it," she told him.

AH, the Glasgow banter. Reader Colin Boyle was on a holiday flight to Alicante when the Glasgow accented steward read the safety instructions, only to end it by stating: "Unfortunately, there will be no alcoholic drinks on the plane today because we forgot to load the right trolley."

The look of stunned disbelief on the coupons of the thirsty sunseekers was a joy to behold until the steward paused for a few seconds before adding: "Only kidding!"

RESPECTED Glasgow cleaning firm boss Eddie Tobin, who was shot on his doorstep by an unknown assailant, was visited in hospital by an old friend who was over on holiday from Australia. "Here, have this," said Eddie who rooted around his possessions – then produced a T-shirt with the logo: "Glasgow. The Friendly City."

A NEW member of the booking staff at Caledonian MacBrayne took down a reservation from a woman whose name on the booking form she wrote as "Karen Driver". It was only afterwards that a colleague pointed out that the woman had, in fact, been trying to book herself and a car on the ferry.

READER Bernie Aspinwall was dining in Florida when he and his companion asked for tea, which came in bags marked NUM. After enjoying the first cuppa they asked for a second.

"Two more Num teas?" asked the waitress. "You wouldn't get away with calling someone that in Glasgow," said Bernie.

13
Getting Back On Your Feet

You might think that the recession is no laughing matter. But in Scotland, you'd be wrong.

FORMER referee Willie Young apologised for being late at a speaking engagement, and said he had broken down twice on the way there.

"I don't have a car," he added. "I'm just very depressed about the state of the economy."

"I GOT a Woolworths' advent calendar," said the schoolboy at the bus stop to his mates.

"All the windows were boarded up, and there was nothing inside."

TALKING of business, Jo Brand, at the Scottish Council for Development and Industry's annual awards dinner in Glasgow, told Scottish business chiefs: "I'm sure you'll all agree that Gordon Brown is creating a lot of small businesses these days."

She added: "Granted they were all large businesses until very recently."

STAFF in a large Edinburgh office were sent an e-mail from the manager's secretary stating that if anyone had lost £40 and could say where they lost it, then to get in touch.

We admire the chap who replied: "On Germany for Euro 2008 at Ladbrokes."

WE HEAR that the children's programme *Bob the Builder* is being renamed because of the recession.

It will now be called *Bob*.

"JOBS are so scarce these days," said the woman in the coffee shop to her friends, "that they even made a programme about it when Sir Alan Sugar gave someone an apprenticeship."

HOW businesses are describing the recession. Phone company Nokia has released a press release about its "synergy-related headcount restructuring".

It's closing a factory and sacking the 500 workers.

INDIAN restaurant magnate Charan Gill says he couldn't help it when a young entrepreneur asked him how he had made his first million. Charan told him: "With my first spare fiver, I bought some chicken

breast and some spices which I turned into a chicken tikka which I sold for £15.

"With the £15, I bought three chicken breasts and spices and sold the three chicken tikkas I made for £45."

"And did you go on doing that until you had made a million?" asked the young chap.

"No," replied Charan, "I kept on doing that until an uncle died and left me three restaurants."

"I HAD terrible financial problems during the credit crunch, but I'm getting back on my feet now," said the chap in the pub.

"My car's been repossessed."

AH, the gallows humour of a recession. Reader Garry Blair brings us news of what has happened to a number of companies recently:

A telephone manufacturing company: called in the receivers.

A firm of bricklayers: gone to the wall.

Flotsam and Jetsam Ltd: washed up.

A tap and sink supply company: pulled the plug.

A ladies' Egyptian dancing school: gone belly-up.

Acme WC drain cleaners: gone down the pan.

A clock and watch repair company: wound up.

"I WENT to the ATM to get cash and it said 'insufficient funds,'" said the chap in the pub.

"And I was wondering – is it them or me?"

WE HEAR a businessman trying to put the FTSE collapse in perspective by explaining to a colleague: "Ten years ago, my shareholdings were worth the equivalent of a brand new BMW sports car.

"Yesterday I checked their value, and they could still buy a 10-year-old BMW, so perhaps the market is finally stabilising."

OUR story about the fisherman who claimed he couldn't live on his net income reminds a reader of the student he knew who had a summer job in a large Glasgow gents' outfitters.

The student jacked it in after a couple of weeks, and appeared to intend no pun when he told folk he left because he wasn't suited.

AN INVESTOR tells us the new definition of liquidity – when you look at the value of your investments, and wet yourself.

NEWS that Marks & Spencer was making more than 1,000 staff redundant, prompted one reader to observe: "This is not just any P45. This P45 is printed on the finest watermarked paper in a crisp white envelope with gorgeously italicised script on the front."

AS THE pound drifts down towards parity with the euro, reader Stewart Smith recalls when Ireland still used the punt in pre-euro days, and Stewart handed over a newly-issued 20 punt note for a round of drinks in a Dublin bar.

The barman looked at the note, with a portrait of a bespectacled James Joyce on it, and announced:

"You've got to be careful with these twenties – there are a lot of forgeries about."

At that he folded the note over and battered it with his fist. He then unfolded it, held it up to the light, and announced: "This one's genuine enough. If it had been a dud, his glasses would be broken."

14
Sport

There can be no mention of politics and religion without that other great Scottish preoccupation – sport.

AN EDINBURGH financial company held its annual golf match for its workforce last week.

One of the older members of staff was playing against a young lad who smashed his first drive just short of the green on the par four.

The older player told him admiringly: "Bloody hell! I don't even go that far on my holidays."

"DID you hear that Gordon Ramsay was being touted as the next Rangers manager?" said the chap in the pub.

"What?" said his mate. "Because he used to play for them before becoming a chef?"

"Naw," his pal replied. "Because he can do wonders with mince."

RETIRED referee Brian McGinlay recalled a match abroad when his linesman was hit by a pomegranate thrown from the crowd, with the match being temporarily halted.

Writing his match report afterwards, Brian wasn't convinced that his spelling of pomegranate was correct, and neither of his linesmen were sure either.

So the match report to Fifa contained: "My linesman was struck on the head with an orange."

FORMER Scotland rugby captain Rob Wainwright told us how players relaxed in his day before a big international.

One Friday evening before a Wales match, the squad visited the cinema, suddenly hearing a commotion from the back seats. In a strong Valleys accent, a young Welsh lady roared: "Get your hands out of my knickers."

The entire cinema went quiet, until a few seconds later the lady concerned said: "No, not you."

ST MIRREN moved to their new ground in the socially deprived area of Ferguslie Park. Reader Ian MacDonald tells us that a St Mirren supporter has already shown the dark humour of Paisley by telling him the nickname of the new stadium is The Methadome.

NEWCASTLE United's sacking of manager Graeme Souness reminds a Celtic fan in Inverness of when Celtic played Souness's previous club, Blackburn Rovers, and a fan ran in front of traffic holding up a home-made banner which declared: "Sounnes is a penis." The fan's pals feared the worst when a local bobby marched over, but the officer merely observed: "You've spelled Souness wrong," and strolled on.

FORMER BBC reporter Bob Wylie recalled Celtic's Uefa Cup final in Seville, and the number of Celtic fans working for Glasgow City Council who applied for holidays to attend the final. Eventually, so many had applied that the council had to say no more time off would be granted.

One chap, said Bob, pleaded his case that he had already booked his flights and, anyway, all the Rangers fans could run things while the Bhoys were away.

But his boss told him not to be so stupid – how could two Rangers fans run the whole council.

A SCOTTISH golf fan attending the Ryder Cup in America told a local golfer where he was from, and the chap replied: "The people who gave us golf and called it a game are the same people who gave us bagpipes and called it music."

DAVID McVey heard a couple of chaps discussing the university boat race returning to BBC television, with one opining: "It's a fix."

When his pal asked why, he replied: "It's always the same two teams in the final."

A READER recalls when four fans turned up at a Motherwell game dressed as the four Teletubby characters – Tinky-Winky, Dipsy, LaaLaa and Po. Being Motherwell though, the four had cards around their necks giving their names as Drinky-Winky, Tipsy, Gaa-gaa and Fu'.

SURELY time for another daft old golf joke, says a reader in a Pringle sweater. Well, what about the married couple who were playing on the ninth green when the chap's wife collapsed with a groan, pleading for help?

Hubby calls 999 on his mobile, talks to a few folk, then picks up his putter to take his shot.

His prostrate wife gasps: "I'm dying over here and you're putting?"

"Don't worry, dear," he replies, "they found a doctor on the second hole and he's coming to help you."

"How long will it take him to get here?" she asks feebly.

"Not long," says her husband. "Everybody's agreed to let him play through."

KILMARNOCK supporters were quick to milk their Scottish Cup win over Ayr United. Fans arriving at Rugby Park for their game against Hamilton Accies could buy special edition T-shirts with the slogan: "We only need 10 men", reflecting the fact the club won even though David Fernandez was sent off. As fans trooped away from the Accies game, in which Kilmarnock suffered a surprise defeat, one fan wearing the new T-shirt was heard arguing: "That'll teach us to play with 11 men."

RALPH Topping, chief executive of multi billion-pound betting firm William Hill's, knows that no matter how tough business gets, it will never be as hair-raising as when he worked as a teenager in a branch in Glasgow's Govan. A punter, upset at a mix-up over which horse he had backed, threatened to end Ralph's relatively short life, before storming out.

Ralph was telling everyone that those who make the loudest threats never carry them out, when the chap returned with a Japanese ceremonial sword with which he slashed at Ralph through the gap below the protective screen.

As 6ft-plus Ralph leapt back from the lethal swipes, his 5ft-nothing Govan cashier went round the front and she bellowed:

"Right, get oot, ya bampot" – which the chap did.

WHEN Gordon Strachan resigned as Celtic manager, and before the new manager was appointed, there was much talk of Strachan not being "Celtic-minded" enough.

So a supporter told us: "The Celtic board is determined to get someone with Irish roots, who has experience of European competitions, as the new manager.

"That's why they've approached Terry Wogan."

THE AYR Gold Cup meeting was a splendid day at the races. However, the combination of betting and drinking all day can lead to a few domestic tiffs.

An Ayrshire taxi driver tells us he was supposed to pick up a couple from the races but when he arrived, the chap's wife jumped in by herself, slammed the door shut on hubby, and shouted out the window to him, in not very friendly terms, that he could walk home.

Five minutes into the journey she orders the driver to stop, and go back for hubby.

"Forgiven him, have you?" asked the driver.

"Naw," she replied. "He's goat the house keys."

WORD reaches us from a boxing gym in Glasgow's east end where the plight of flawed boxing champ Scott Harrison is being discussed. "He's finished with boxing and is going to take up tennis," says one pugilist. When his fellow fighters express surprise at this, he delivers the punch line. "Aye," he tells them, "Scott's been in more courts than Martina Navratilova."

MISSING apostrophes often offend our readers. One Diary reader who was at the Celtic game at the weekend noticed that one bold Celtic fan had painted his own wee banner – which would have been far more positive if it had included the missing apostrophe. Instead the red-painted banner had the more pessimistic declaration: "Were Magic".

JOHN Motson, the English football commentator who has retired from covering internationals, always irked Scottish football fans with his knack of mentioning England's 43-year-old World Cup win at every turn.

As one fan opined in the pub at the weekend: "If I wanted someone constantly to interrupt my enjoyment of the fitba' with stupid, pointless, rambling, ill-informed comment, then I'd get a girlfriend."

WE HEAR about the Queen of the South fan who got lost in Glasgow going to the Scottish Cup Final at Hampden against Rangers last season. He eventually arrived a quarter of an hour late. His pals have now nicknamed him the Big Game Hunter.

TOM Gallacher recalled when he played for Dalry Thistle in the 1980s and the team faced Irvine Meadow in a cup semi-final which went to penalties.

Only four players volunteered to take them, so the manager turned to the captain and asked if he would step up. But he replied: "No, I don't fancy taking one."

The irate manager told him: "I was hoping for something a bit more positive."

"OK," replied the skipper. "I definitely don't fancy taking one."

A BAFFLED punter overheard by reader Keith Murray outside a Glasgow pub on Saturday: "A hundred-to-one shot winnin' the Grand National. What's the odds o' that?"

FORMER Celtic and St Mirren star Frank McAvennie pitched up at old St Mirren mate Billy Abercromby's autobiography launch at Braehead and told waiting fans of the time Aber turned up at a club night out in Glasgow wearing a sheepskin jacket and slippers.

Explained Frank: "When we asked Billy why he was wearing slippers, he told us he had been walking his dog and had suddenly remembered about the night out.

"Billy had legged it straight from his dogwalking to the nightclub and when we asked where the dog was, Billy said he just put it on the bus and asked the driver to let it off at the next stop."

"I FELT really sick after using the new machine they've installed at the gym," the young woman was telling her pal over a relaxing bottle of rioja in the pub on Friday night.

"Was it a running machine?" her pal asked.

"No," replied the gym-goer. "A new vending machine full of KitKats and Crunchies."

A POWER failure at Celtic Park meant fans waiting in the cold for nearly an hour before the game commenced. One chap in the Jock Stein stand noticed that his girlfriend was shaking with the cold and her lips were turning blue. He stood up and started to escort her out of the stand and the concerned chap next to him asked: "Are you taking her to hospital?"

"Naw," the chap replied. "I thought we could sit in the car with the heater on, listening to the game on the radio until she warms up."

CELTIC legend Bobby Lennox being inducted into the Hampden Hall of Fame, reminded Paul O'Sullivan of when Bobby was stretchered off an Old Firm game with a broken leg following a bruising tackle from Rangers captain John Greig. Propped up in the Western Infirmary that evening with his leg in plaster Bobby was being interviewed for *Scotsport* when the reporter asked Bobby when he realised his leg was broken. With a straight face, Bobby replied: "When I saw John Greig running towards me."

ONE of the first people to buy a copy of Celtic footballer Neil Lennon's autobiography, *Man And Bhoy*, was BBC sports reporter Chick Young, which might raise an eyebrow as he is often portrayed as a Rangers man, although Chick will tell you he follows St Mirren.

A smiling Neil at the book-signing in the Celtic Superstore asked Chick who he should make out the dedication to.

"To the lucky winner on e-Bay," replied Chick.

15
Women Who Lunch

The big change in Scotland is the number of financially independent women who like nothing better than a laugh when they meet their pals for a drink or a coffee. These are some of their stories.

THE CENTRE of Glasgow was assailed by large numbers of ladies-who-lunch seeking further refreshment after a charity lunch at the Hilton. One chap in a smart bar was approached by one such lady who gently swayed in front of him and told him: "You look like my third husband."

"Bloody hell," he told her. "How many husbands have you had?"

"Two," she replied.

A FORTYSOMETHING lady who lunches out with her friends in a Glasgow city centre restaurant, was not impressed by her tired-looking chocolate cake. She sniffed it and declared: "It smells like cocoa."

The smug waiter told her: "It's chocolate cake. It should smell like cocoa."

"Coco's my dog," she replied.

THE YOUNG woman ordering the large white wine took a large gulp before telling her pal: "That idiot boss of mine said I would get a pay rise when I earned it."

After another slurp she added: "If he thinks I'm going to wait that long, he's got another think coming."

THE WOMAN collecting a bottle of prosecco in the Glasgow bar, settled down at her table and asked her pal how her blind date had gone the previous weekend.

"Terrible," her pal replied. "He picked me up in a vintage Rolls-Royce." "What's wrong with that?" asked her mate.

"He was the original owner," she replied.

"I DON'T gossip myself," confided the woman in the Glasgow coffee shop to her friend.

"But I do like to pass on snippets to people who do," she added.

"THE ONLY way my husband would put me on a pedestal," exclaimed the woman sharing a bottle of wine with her friends, "would be if he wanted the ceiling painted."

WE WATCHED as three ladies-who-lunch in Glasgow's Princes Square each tried to take the bill from the waiter after they had dined together. "Give it to me," said one.

"No, you got it last time," said another. "I'll get it."

The poor waiter was completely confused until the third perfectly-coiffured lady declared: "I'm the biggest tipper," and the bill was swiftly placed before her.

A WEST END woman gulping down a large pinot grigio after a day at the office opined: "Well, if it's not one thing, it's another."

Her friend, stirring her Hendriks gin and tonic, replied: "Or as my therapist puts it, 'If it's not one thing, it's your mother.'"

A GROUP of ladies having a post-shopping drink in Glasgow's west end were discussing the complexities of their mobile phone agreements, which seemed so attractive when they took them out.

"I got out of my marriage," declared one of them, "easier than getting out of my mobile phone contract."

"SHE'S that stupid," said a woman chatting about a mutual friend in a west end bar, "that she probably throws breadcrumbs in the toilet bowl to feed the toilet duck."

THE YOUNG woman meeting her pals for a cocktail after work one Friday posed the question:

"What do you call a magic wand that makes a man quickly disappear?"

When her pals all shook their heads, she told them: "A home pregnancy test."

WE OVERHEAR the women in the wine bar discussing a mutual friend, with one of them declaring: "She's not as promiscuous as you make out. She told me she could count on one hand all the men she had slept with."

"Was she holding a calculator at the time?" asked the more world-weary of the party.

A WOMAN in the Marks & Spencer food hall was chatting to a pal about a mutual friend when she declared: "I wouldn't say she was cynical, but if she smelled flowers she would look round for the funeral."

"I LEFT my job because of illness and fatigue," we hear a woman in a coffee shop tell her pals. She adds: "My boss got sick and tired of me."

A WOMAN having coffee with her friend announced: "My ex-husband wants to marry me again."

"That's very flattering," said her pal.

"Not really," replied the woman. "I think he's just after the money I married him for."

WE OVERHEAR a woman telling her pal, when asked about her boyfriend, that he had "issues".

She went on to explain what they were until her pal interrupted: "Issues? Sounds like he's got a year's subscription."

"I WANT my children to have all the things I never could afford," declared the woman having coffee with her friends in a city centre patisserie.

"And then I'm going to move in with them."

WE OVERHEAR a west end woman having a catch-up pinot grigio with an old friend tell her that she had recently ended a long-term relationship.

When her pal expressed some sympathy, the lady replied: "Oh, no, not mine. The guy I met had been going steady with someone for more than a year."

TWO ladies dining in Pintxo's tapas restaurant in Glasgow's west end were discussing the love life of a mutual friend. "She's been on so many blind dates," one of them declared, "she should qualify for a free dog."

THE WOMAN ordering up a giant meringue in Fifi and Ally's coffee shop in Glasgow was easily overheard as she told her pal: "So I just said to my boss, 'There's something I'd like to get off my chest.'

"When he asked, 'What?' I told him, 'Your eyes.'"

WE OVERHEAR a woman in a west end coffee shop tell her pal: "I've taken up meditation . . . well, it beats sitting around doing nothing."

16
Pub

Drink, rightly or wrongly, often plays a role in Scottish life. Here are some tales which slip down easily.

NEWS from the Scottish smoking ban. Reader Dougie Timmins was drinking in the Enigma bar in Coatbridge, which has a sign outside boasting that it now had its own gazebo in the beer garden – so that smokers could light up no matter the weather – when a woman walked in with a toddler asking where the gazebo was.

When Dougie directed her out the back she returned minutes later to say she couldn't see the gazebo. Being the helpful sort, he went outside, showed her the newly-built awning when she suddenly slapped her forehead and told him: "I was thinking zebra. Ah wanted a picture of ma wean with it."

WE HEAR about a stag night in Newcastle where the Scottish chaps end up in a casino watching a fellow player making a killing with the black £25 chips piling up in front of him.

"Ah huvnae seen that many black chips," said a member of the stag from Ayrshire, "since ma' last fish supper in Saltcoats."

LEADING Glasgow solicitor Paul Reid was keen to show that it's not just when they are making up their fees that lawyers show a sense of humour. So he enrolled on a 10-week course in stand-up comedy before making his debut in front of an audience at a bar in Shettleston in Glasgow's east end.

As he told the locals when he walked on stage: "I hear this pub is so tough that the first question in the pub quiz is, 'Who the **** are you looking at?' "

RONNIE Bulloch, sales executive at Inverarity Vaults, who won the Achievement Award at the inaugural Òran Mór Whisky Awards in Glasgow, bemoaned the fact that there were fewer characters in the drinks trade these days. He recalled a rep from Tennent's going into a bar in Glasgow's down-to-earth Gallowgate and being told by the owner that he feared he might lose his licence.

When the rep asked why, the owner told him there had been a fight on the premises on Friday night.

As this was a regular occurrence, the rep reassured him that he shouldn't lose his livelihood over it.

"The police were in," the owner continued, but again the rep tried to reassure him it was a common enough occurrence for police to be needed.

"No' wi' horses they're no," replied the glum owner.

WE ARE told of a chap in a Glasgow city centre bar who looked at his freshly poured pint then complained to the barman that it was cloudy.

We are still trying to check that the barman really replied: "What do you expect for two pound fifty? Thunder and lightning?"

A READER in Bar Budda in Glasgow's West End overheard a couple of chaps discussing the bar's televised football policy with one declaring: "They always show the Celtic games in here, but when there's a Rangers game on the telly you have to ask them to put it to the right channel."

"Maybe this is a Celtic pub," said his mate.

"Aye, maybe. Was Buddha a Catholic?"

"Dunno mate, must have been," he replied.

"TWO POUNDS a week will supply water for an entire village in Malawi, according to Christian Aid," says a bar-room philosopher in a west-end pub at the weekend. "So how come Scottish Water charges me nearly £20 a month to supply a flat in Partick? The fleecing shysters."

"WAIT a minute," said the chap in the bar the other night. "Have I already told you my déjà vu joke?"

GLASGOW southside boulevardier Jack McLean was most put out when he went in to the Granary bar in Shawlands and was asked to remove his trademark fedora. It seems that bars with CCTV want customers to be bareheaded so that they can be identified if they cause trouble.

It is aimed, it has to be said, to hoodie or baseball cap-wearing troublemakers rather than elegant chaps in fedoras.

Jack's telling remark to the barmaid, "So I suppose you wouldn't serve Humphrey Bogart in here?", lost much of its impact when she asked who Humphrey was.

THE Griffin Bar in Glasgow has written on its menu: "Warning. The Griffin Bar Menu. May contain nuts."

The word menu has been neatly scored out.

WINE expert David Morgan was explaining to the Glasgow Wine and Dine Club that a major study had discovered that the average time from buying a bottle of wine with a metal screw-top to actually opening it is not weeks, months or years, but only 17 minutes.

"Was the study solely confined to Glasgow?" asked one of the wine aficionados.

"I GOT a job fixing sheets of wood over broken windows," said the chap in the pub the other night.

"All those years at boarding school have finally paid off."

A FESTIVE clubber in Glasgow tells us he was waiting in a busy pre-new year queue when a steward, in an unusual seasonal bout of goodwill, told a chap at the front who was a trifle unsteady on his feet: "Go and get a cup of coffee and we'll think about letting you in." The chap wandered over to a nearby snack caravan and returned with a cup of coffee which he handed to the steward with the request: "There you go pal, can I get in now?"

REPORTING from Oldhall in Paisley, Diary stalwart Donald Grant assures us he was in a trendy pub when he overheard a young man-about-town trying to impress a young lady by listing his many skills. He concluded by asserting: "Ah also huv a magnetic personality."

Says Donald: "Without even turning her head she dismissed him with the words 'Then, if ah wis you, ah'd steer well clear o' scrapyards."

WITHERING putdowns, continued. Tom Nugent, of Troon, remembers working at the Singer factory in Clydebank where gate security was intense to prevent petty theft of parts. A young lady seen leaving with a large cardboard box was targeted by a rotund security man who bellowed: "Haw, whit's that ye've goat under yer airm?"

Without breaking stride, she replied: "Hair. Whit have you goat under yours?"

A GLASGOW GP, who had been a trombone player in his spare time, was asked to join a big band, and knowing that one of his patients, now in his eighties, had been a professional saxophone player, he asked his patient next time he was in if he had any tips about playing in such a group.

He was hoping for suggestions on playing technique, but instead the auld fella told him:

"When the fightin' starts, play a waltz.

"They cannae fight tae a waltz."

TALES of wedding guests nipping out from expensive hotels for a cheap drink from their cars reminds Isobel MacDonald of a friend on Arran who went to a wedding reception with a beautifully wrapped present which she sat on the table.

Only the most eagle-eyed spotted that it was in fact a carefully wrapped wine box from which she discreetly topped up her glass all evening, before disposing of the then empty box in the bin, leaving none of the hotel staff any the wiser.

"HE'S SO tightfisted," declared the chap in the Glasgow pub the other night, discussing a mutual friend, "that if he came home early and saw a plumber's van outside his house, he'd hope his wife was having an affair."

WE OVERHEAR one bar-room philosopher looking at his glass of whisky and declaring: "Alcohol doesn't solve any problems."

He then swallowed it down before adding: "But then again, neither does milk."

SO THE guy in the pub declares: "I once lived in a very rough part of town – it was so bad I had to go home every night by the local super-market as it was the only Morrisons."

As his companions looked at him in puzzlement, he took another swallow of his beer, then added: "Of course, that worked better as a gag when it was called Safeway."

"HE'S that thick," said the chap in the bar while discussing a mutual friend, "he thinks a bigamist is a heavy fog around Naples."

CHEEKY barstaff, continued. Jim Scott was in a bar in Girvan when two old worthies came in, with one asking: "Gie's two Grouse."

The barman replied: "Ma feet are killing me and I hate folk who don't say please and thank you."

A DRUNK weaving out of a bar spots a minister walking past and immediately announces to him that he is Jesus Christ. The minister tries to calm him down by telling him he is mistaken, but the drunk is adamant.

"Here, I can prove it to you," he says, taking the minister by the arm and leading him into the bar he has just left.

The barman looks up and says: "Jesus Christ. Not you again."

THE CHIP in the West End's Ashton Lane has a narrow flight of stairs up to the first floor bar. From there is another tricky set of steps up to the roof terrace. Heading up there for a drink the other day was a chap who had bought two tyres for his mountain bike, which he propped up on either side of his roof terrace chair while sipping his pint. Eventually a chap detached himself from a group nearby having

an earnest discussion, and sidled up to the tyre buyer to ask: "Sorry to bother you, but me and my mates cannot work out how you managed to get your wheelchair up here."

FURTHER news of the Glasgow pubs crowded out on Friday as office workers finished up for Christmas. One chap who was getting a round in realised that he was stuck with buying drinks for eight or nine folk. As the barman started ringing up all the drinks on the till, the poor chap shouted at him: "That's not a bloody piano you're playing."

WE SUPPOSE he couldn't resist it, the chap in the West Lothian bar who asked for an orange juice. The barmaid turned away, hesitated, then turned back and asked: "Still orange?"

And he replied: "Yes, I've not changed my mind."

ALASTAIR Bilsland tells us that some years ago a group of Arran lads who had sailed over for the Cowal games were returning to their small boat tied up at Dunoon pier when they noticed that a rubbish bin on the pier had been set alight and the conflagration was threatening to spread to the pier itself. One of the Arran lads rushed into the pier-head disco which was in full swing and shouted at the barman: "Quick – get me a fire extinguisher." "Certainly sir," replied the barman, "Is that a vodka based one or a gin based one?"

TALES of bar staff remind Ian Glasgow of being a young, inexperienced barman on Jersey when a customer asked for a screwdriver.

Says Ian: "I now know it to be vodka and orange juice, but on that occasion I refused the customer because, coming from Glasgow, I thought he needed it to jemmy the fag machine."

ALLAN Kelly in Perth recalls a charge-hand, when Allan worked as a student barman, who bought large bottles of mixers from the wholesalers, and after hours would refill the mixer baby bottles already used and refit the bottle tops from the bin, straightening them where necessary.

Added Allan: "The next day he would then charge full price and pocket the takings. Of course the flaw in his strategy was that the mixers went flat overnight as the bottles were not sealed properly, but he fixed this by looking away and making a 'psshht' sound as he opened them."

"I USED to dress off the peg," declared the chap in the pub to his mates. "But now my neighbours don't leave their washing out at night."

17
Barking Mad

DO WE believe the jeweller in the Argyll Arcade who claims that a distraught woman came in with a picture of her recently deceased dog, and asked if a gold statue of it could be made so that she would have a permanent reminder of her faithful companion?

He says he asked her: "Eighteen carat?"

And she replied: "No, chewing a bone."

A READER was passing a woman returning to her car, in which her dog was sitting, and heard her declare as she looked at the panting pooch: "It's not that hot. Stop faking it."

A HERALD feature on dealing with a pet's bereavement reminded Jim Thomson in Irvine of the mother having to tell her eight-year-old son that Laddie the labrador had died during the night.

Instead of the expected floods of tears and broken heart, there was a quiet acceptance and off to school he went with a kiss and a hug.

On his return the first thing he asked was: "Where's Laddie?" Mum told him again that Laddie had died. Now the tears and awful sobs ensued.

Eventually she asked why he hadn't been sad in the morning. He replied: "I thought you said Daddy!"

WE DOUBT very much that someone went into a pet shop to buy a goldfish and when the assistant asked: "Do you want an aquarium?" replied:

"I really don't care what star sign it is."

AS CHILDREN begin their campaigns to get a puppy or kitten for Christmas, we are told by one reader that when he was much younger he pestered his parents for a cat but was always told no.

Then when a mate's cat had kittens he took one home, pausing only to pour water over it, then went in claiming he had rescued it when someone threw it in the river in a sack.

His mother bought the story, and the kitten stayed.

A READER hears the woman sitting in front of him on the bus tell her pal:

"We got a new cat. We thought the little one would like it."

"Is it a tom?" asked her pal.

"Of course," replied her pal. "I'm hardly likely to bring it into town with me, am I?"

ALLAN Thomson in Glasgow claims that a friend of his went into a Glasgow pet shop looking for a yellow canary, and the store owner offered her a green budgie instead.

"That's not what I'm looking for," his friend replied.

But the pet shop-owner persisted: "Just think of it as a yellow canary that's not quite ripe yet."

A PUPPY bought by an Ayrshire couple for their daughters received lots of care and attention, especially from the dad. One night his wife came home, watched him lovingly stroke the dog's chin, and asked: "What do I need to do to have my chin stroked like that?"

"Bark," he replied.

18
Second to none

Scots pride themselves on their warm welcome to foreign visitors – even though mutual understanding is sometimes missing.

READER David Baillie was at the Edinburgh Military Tattoo, enthralled by the Swiss army drummers whose complicated and fast routine received a rousing response from the crowd. As the applause died down, a chap behind him declared: "You can certainly tell the armies with time on their hands."

THE POPULAR Ben Nevis in Glasgow's west end has a new Polish barman who comes from a country where civil partnerships among same-sex couples are still unknown.

Two west end chaps ordered up a bottle of champagne in the Ben Nevis and told the Pole that they were celebrating getting married the following Tuesday.

"Coincidence," replied the barman. "Both on the same day."

SPOTTED in Kosovo, a large sign outside a US army base which, in the flamboyant military manner of our transatlantic cousins, announced the location of a unit claiming to be "Second To None".

A mile down the road, the sign outside a usually understated British base was hastily changed to "None".

WE VERY much admire Aussie plain speaking. Retired Aussie diplomat Richard Woolcott tells of former Australian Prime Minister Bob Hawke leaving his Japanese audience bewildered when he used the Australian colloquial phrase "I am not here to play funny buggers" after he was asked what he thought was a cheeky question.

The Japanese translator told the audience Bob had replied: "I am not here to play laughing homosexuals with you."

AN AMERICAN swears blind to us that he was having lunch while on holiday in Scotland, and when the bill came he told the waiter that, unfortunately, he only had enough in cash to pay the total but would have nothing left for a tip.

"Let me add that up again, sir," the waiter replied.

DENNIS Kelly was in a Prestwick Airport restaurant queue when a young Japanese tourist nervously pointed at the sausages behind the glass counter, and was then asked by the buxom Ayrshire lady serving him: "Mash?"

Says Dennis: "He looked even more nervous now, and as he was obviously stuck, she tried to help him by increasing her volume and saying, 'D'ye want mash wi' that?'

"Seeing how panic-stricken he now looked, she again tried to help by saying, 'Mash, ye ken, tatties, mashed tatties.' At that point the young man took his sausages and fled."

Adds Dennis: "Who says we Scots are not a helpful people?"

AN AMERICAN who arrived at Glasgow Airport was asked at immigration: "Occupation?"

"No," he replied. "Just visiting."

IAIN Emerson, editor of the famous *Tartan Army* magazine, which was shortlisted in the Periodical Publishers' Association's Scottish awards, tells us they were contacted by a young lad in Kenya who e-mailed the magazine about his love of football. So the chaps at the mag posted him off a few issues of their publication.

The young lad e-mails back weeks later to thank them — and reveals he is doing a roaring trade renting them out to Scottish squaddies on duty in the country.

A READER swears he was in an Edinburgh hotel at New Year when an American guest, obviously keen to do a bit of keep-fit while he was here, asked the receptionist: "Do you have a weight room?"

Clearly not on the same wavelength, she replied: "No, but you can always wait here in reception."

A READER who has returned from a trip to Rome heard two Italians chatting up a couple of young women whom he could tell were from Glasgow by their accents.

One of the Italians was perhaps going overboard in telling one of the girls how beautiful she was. "In my country, you would be a princess," he was telling her.

Not overly impressed, she replied: "And in my country you'd be selling ice-cream. Now beat it."

OUR story of the foreign cleaner who was struggling to understand the Scots word "stoor" reminds Rob Parker in Edinburgh of when he was playing in a football tournament in America, and his team's manager, a Glaswegian, felt that after a stoppage the referee should be restarting the game with a dropped ball rather than conceding a free kick to the opposition.

Rob still recalls the blustering, red-faced manager screaming at the referee: "It's a stoat up! Stoat it! Stoat the baw!"

"Needless to say," says Rob, "the confused referee merely smiled and got on with the game."

THE NEWS story about the chap who was visiting every place named Glasgow in America reminds Paul Drury, boss of Glasgow PR firm Media Now, of his previous life as a newspaper reporter and being sent on an assignment to Kentucky.

On a whim, he visited Glasgow, Kentucky, population 14,000, where the waitress in the steak house was taken with his accent, as they didn't get many visitors.

Says Paul: "When she asked where we came from, we said Scotland,

and I went further, telling her that not only did we come from Scotland but that we came from Glasgow in Scotland.

"She replied, 'Gee, you mean there's another one?'"

AH, the Glasgow banter. Reader Des Divers was on the Glasgow to Edinburgh train when a group of chaps on a stag night engaged two Dutch girls in conversation. They were discussing why so many people used bicycles in Holland when one of the chaps asked why the bikes he saw in Holland were in such a bad state. One of the Dutch girls said that if your bicycle was ugly nobody would ever bother wanting to steal it. Immediately one of the chaps told her: "That's how I picked my wife."

A JOURNALIST on one of the smaller radio stations in Scotland tells us of the day when a bulletin contained a particularly difficult surname of a Polish chap who was injured in a car accident locally. Staff were taking childish pleasure in whether the bumptious newsreader would stumble over it. But when it came to the name, the newsreader smoothly announced: "The driver's name has been withheld by police until relatives have been informed."

19
Worth a Study

All of Glasgow's cities are now hoaching with students, and the daftness of student life is worth recording.

GLASGOW'S Professor Jason Ditton told a newspaper investigating exam plagiarism, in which students cut and paste material from the internet, that when he was an external university examiner, one student's essay was spotted as a cheat because it ended with the phrase: "For more information, click here."

WE HEAR about a Milngavie teenager who left home to move into a student flat in Glasgow last year, who asked his mum how to cook a meal as he had a new girlfriend coming round to the apartment for dinner.

Afterwards his mum phoned to ask how the meal went, and her son told her: "Not so great. She wanted to wash the dishes."

"What's wrong with that?" asked his mum.

"It was before I'd served the food," he explained.

WE ARE told about the Edinburgh couple who were trying to persuade their student son to come with them to visit his gran at the weekend, but the chap was whining that he didn't want to go as he had nothing in common with the old lady.

"I don't know about that," his dad told him. "You both take drugs, and I would never let either of you drive my car."

A DAD tells us his teenage daughter had left school and was applying for a job to tide her over before going to college. Under "previous employment" he encouraged her to put "babysitting", to show that she at least had a work ethic.

When he was checking the form for her later, he noticed that after putting in babysitter, the form asked "reason for leaving", and his daughter had written: "They came home."

OUR exam-paper stories remind David Currie of the student who was finding the going difficult, and drops of sweat from his forehead fell on to his exam paper.

Hoping to convince the lecturer how hard he was working, he outlined the droplets in blue ink, writing "sweat" next to them.

But when his exam paper was returned with a score below the pass mark, the circles were now marked in red with the word "tears" beside them.

A GLASGOW school-leaver who attended a prestigious university for an interview tells us that, on reflection, he probably gave the wrong answer when he was asked: "If you could have dinner with someone alive or dead, who would it be?" and he replied without thinking: "The alive one."

A GLASGOW University student reminiscing on his first year, was recalling the nerve-racking process of trying to make friends. While at his halls of residence's Freshers Week party, he overheard one girl initiate conversation with the obligatory: "What are you studying?" The chap being questioned replied: "Pharmacology." "You're kidding," screeched the girl excitedly, "I used to work on a farm!"

AND IAN Sutherland remembers striking up a conversation in Corfu with a Scottish barmaid when he was a student and she asking him what he was studying.

"Parasitology," he replied.

She paused for a good few seconds before asking: "Do you need to go to France for that?"

POLITICIAN Dennis Canavan, being presented with an honorary doctorate at Stirling University, told the students that he had met former Rangers captain John Greig after he had been given an honorary doctorate from Glasgow University. But when Dennis said: "Congratulations, John," he growled: "What do you mean by that?"

It turned out that as Rangers had just been beaten by Euro minnows Kaunas, John thought Dennis was being sarcastic.

Continued Dennis: "I hastily explained to John that I was congratulating him on his doctorate.

"Whereupon John said, 'Ach well, Dennis, ye ken whit it's like.
They're giein' them away tae onybody these days.'"

WE OVERHEAR a student tell his pals: "When I left home my mum
told me, 'Don't forget to write.'

"But I thought, 'How would anyone forget such a basic skill as
that'?"

TALKING of students at their first job interview, one reader tells us
that when he was at uni, job-hunting, he was asked by an interviewer:
"What's your ultimate goal?"

On reflection, he thinks his reply of "Archie Gemmell's against Holland in the World Cup" may have contributed to him not getting the
job.

OUR tales questioning young folk's worldly knowledge lead to a lecturer
at one of the newer universities claiming that, when he discussed the
Second World War with his first-year students, one of them asked
afterwards why he "kept going on about the dog in the insurance
advert".

WE OVERHEAR a group of students discussing the virtues of buying
a high-definition television screen. "My mum came round to the flat

and turned our ordinary TV into a high-definition one," declared one of them.

When asked how she managed that, he told his pals: "She ran a duster over it."

A STUDENT in Glasgow's Campus bar was telling his pals about the letter he sent to his gran, thanking her for the cheque for thirty quid she had sent him at Christmas. He told her he'd spent it on a jumper. "It seemed the easiest way of saying I'd opened an online account with Ladbrokes," he told his mates.

A LECTURER at Glasgow Uni who has been marking dissertations gives us the real explanation of phrases frequently used.

- "It has long been known" – I didn't look up the original reference.
- "Three of the samples were chosen for detailed study" – the other results didn't make any sense.
- "It is believed that" – I think.
- "It is generally believed that" – my flatmates agree with me.
- "According to statistical analysis" – rumour has it.

20
Daughter's Day

I love kids – I just couldn't eat a whole one is the old gag about children. But in Scotland they are truly loved, as these stories show.

A READER tells us he took his family for a special meal at a country-house hotel which had mounted stags' heads in the foyer. One of them had a couple of party hats hanging from its antlers.

Noticing his young daughter had stopped walking and was staring at the head, he told her that unfortunately some folk liked to hunt animals.

"But why did they have to shoot him on his birthday?" she wailed.

GLASGOW'S hackney cab drivers take disadvantaged children to Troon every year in a fleet of ballooned and decorated Glasgow cabs. One driver tells of a previous year's trip when a group of taxis arrived to pick up children from a school with handicapped pupils who were helped into the cabs. As he waited with half a dozen other cabs, the door opened and a woman popped two children inside.

Driving off in the convoy, the chatty driver asked them how long they had been pupils at the school.

"Oh, we don't go there," one replied. "But our ma thought it would be a great day out for us."

And as he was already on his way to Troon, the driver carried on, reluctantly admiring the woman's cheek.

READER Marion Husband recalls her time in a maternity ward when the girl in the next bed proudly told her visiting granny that she was giving the baby the somewhat exotic name for Glasgow of Che.

But the granny's reaction was: "Ye canny call the wean Che. There's an Alsatian dug in oor street called that."

READER Norman Brown in Barassie tells us of a friend who was asked by his five-year-old son: "Daddy, what does baws mean?"

The shocked parent replied that it was not a very nice word, he was never to say it again and, anyway, where had he heard it?

"Mummy," his son replied. "Every night she says it's time for beddy-baws."

"I TOLD my kids," said the loudmouth in the bar, "that when I was their age, all I got at Christmas was an orange and an apple.

"But all my son said was, 'Wow, a mobile phone and a computer – not bad.'"

READER Campbell Laird, of Greenock, reveals that his seven-year-old niece, Nina, shocked her grandmother by complaining: "Mum said the F-word to my brother Shaun."

Pressed further, Nina explained to her disbelieving granny exactly what it was her mum had said: "Shaun wanted to go out to play and mum said, 'Forget it.'"

AN AYRSHIRE reader was being quizzed by his eight-year-old grandson about the Second World War, and the youngster seemed surprised at the news that his grandad had no television in those days.

"No telly?" said the youngster. "Did you just text your friends?" he asked.

A WEST end parent finds his two young daughters trying to get the pet guinea pig out from behind a dresser. One of them is kneeling at one end with a carrot while the other daughter is at the other end trying to poke it out with a broom handle.

It was the first time, he realised, that he had actually ever seen someone use the old carrot and stick approach to a problem.

PROOF that technology is changing quicker than you realise. A reader in a Paisley office overheard a colleague during the school summer holidays on the phone to her daughter, telling her: "I think we have it on tape . . . on tape. Video tape.

"No, not a DVD. Video. Black plastic box you put in the VCR.

"VCR? Look it's, no, just wait till I get home OK?"

A READER visiting an overly protective couple was asked if she made sure that she shut the garden gate behind her as they did not want their four-year-old, playing in the garden with her Christmas toys, getting out on to the road.

The couple must have really drummed the message into their daughter as she came dashing into the house shouting: "Quick, Mum! The gate's open and I might get out!"

WE ARE told about the couple trying to console their young son when the family pet dog died, with mum telling him: "It's not so bad. Prince is probably up in heaven right now, having a grand old time with God."

Their son stopped sobbing long enough to ask: "What would God want with a dead dog?"

A YOUNG Coatbridge girl, enthused by the television talent show *Britain's Got Talent*, ran to her dad and asked if she could enter next year.

"Aye, no problem," he said from behind his newspaper.

"What do you think I should do?" she persisted. "Sing or a comedy act?" "What's the difference?" was the unhelpful reply from behind the paper.

A READER tells us she may have regrets about her husband always driving their children to school in the morning. When she picked up her five-year-old recently she passed the time by quizzing him on traffic lights, and asked what the red light stood for.

"Stop," he said. "And green?" "Go," he replied. "Amber?" she asked. "Hold on," he said.

A HARASSED mother at Mearns shopping centre in Renfrewshire was asked by her trailing daughter: "Mummy. When's Mother's Day?"

"March," she replied.

"And is there a Daughter's Day?" her little one asked.

"The other 364 days," replied her mum.

A GLASGOW mother who had been out shopping all day had left her son at her sister's. When she arrived to collect him, the little lad told her proudly: "I've been a good boy today."

"You can't get into much trouble lying on the couch all day," his aunt explained.

"Dad does," the little one replied.

A READER in Knightswood, Glasgow, out for a stroll in the good weather, sees a child attempting to manoeuvre the family lawnmower which had been left out in the garden.

The child's mother spots him and shouts something our reader agrees is very true: "If that mower cuts aff yer toes, don't come running to me."

A YOUNG woman sheltering from the downpour in a Glasgow city centre shop door was pushing a double buggy with twins inside.

An older woman sheltering beside her raved on about how lovely the two nippers were, how beautiful they looked sleeping, before telling the young woman: "You're very lucky."

"I am," the young buggy-pusher replied. "They're ma sister's."

A FATHER managed to keep his face straight when his teenage daughter was pleading to have a pony, and her mother, claiming it was too expensive, told her that the pony would need new shoes every six weeks.

"No different from you, then, mum," replied the feisty teenager.

A READER in the queue at a Glasgow sandwich shop heard the harassed mother next to him ask for a glass of water to go with her young daughter's sandwich.

"But ah want a Coke!" the little girl screeched.

"It's OK," said the mother winking at the assistant, "it's Coke water."

At that the little girl went "Yes!" and happily sat down.

SHOWING that children do have a point at times, a mother tells us that she was talking about a burst pipe further down the road and how "raw sewage was flowing in the gutter". Her daughter piped up: "Raw sewage? Don't tell me people cook it?"

WEEGIE exile in Edinburgh Margaret Fowler remembers her daughter asking: "How old are you, granny" and being told by Margaret's mum: "Sweetheart, I'm as old as Methuselah."

This information was digested before the young girl asked: "But granny, how old is your thuselah?"

DAVID Macleod told his then six-year-old son off for bad behaviour and added: "Right . . . that's it! No McDonald's for you today."

They walked on in silence for a while before his son piped up: "Dad, see instead of not going to McDonald's . . . can I not go to the Thistle game instead?"

A MUM was impressed by the manners of the little girl who arrived at her daughter's sixth birthday party and chirruped as she came in the door: "In case I forget, I'd like to say that I had a very nice time."

A MUM tells us that her husband had taken their young son to work one day, as the company had encouraged parents to bring their children to an open day.

The little one looked really disappointed when he came home, and when she asked him why, he told her: "I never got to see the clowns dad said he worked with."

21
Three Yards of a Start

Work is the curse of the drinking classes, as the old saying goes, but humour is never far away from the work-place.

A GLASGOW chap working for an international company had to attend a staff meeting where a motivational speaker was telling them how they could fulfil their potential.

An air-conditioning unit in the corner was clunking away making a bit of a racket, however, and the speaker finally asked: "Is that noise annoying you as much as me?" "No, I think you just edge it," muttered a voice from the back of the room.

A DIARY reader tells us about his ex-wife being interviewed for a job, and when she was asked: "Do you have any convictions?" she replied: "I'm strongly against seal hunting."

OUR MENTION of job interviews reminds Joe Mullen of an electrician pal who went for a job interview just before Christmas one year. He was told by the young interviewer that nothing was available at present, but added: "Why don't you come back in the spring?"

The interviewee replied: "Son, I'm an electrician, not a bloody daffodil."

OUR STORY of the chap writing "five miles" on the application form under "nearest relative" reminds Dr Jim Rodgers in Kelso of when he worked in the west of Scotland and had to countersign an Italian fishshop worker's claim form after an accident.

In the section "Occupation (If Self-Employed give a description)" the chap had written: "Small, baldy with a moustache."

A READER tells us about the time he worked in a meat-processing factory when the woman in front of him, who was a bit bulky it has to be said, suddenly dropped a large ham from under her voluminous skirt as she was walking past the gate security staff.

He admired her aplomb as she turned to the staff walking out behind her and shouted: "Right! Which wan o' youse chucked that at me?"

WITH all the interest in the history of the Clyde, Jim McDonald in Carluke remembers when he started as an apprentice at Fairfield Shipbuilders, in Govan, and was soon challenged by his journeyman to take part in the annual race between journeymen and the apprentices, from Govan Cross to Shieldhall. Knowing how fit the apprentices were, he asked what the catch was, but was told there was no catch – all the journeymen wanted was three yards of a start.

It was a while before the penny dropped that the three yards the journeymen had in mind were Harland & Wolff, Fairfields and Alexander Stephen and Sons.

GLASGOW landscape painter Ed Hunter, whose atmospheric canvasses are regularly exhibited in west of Scotland galleries, worked in housing before taking a redundancy package and becoming a full-time artist. When he was making his farewells to steering group members in Ruchazie, he was in the local fruit shop, where the owner said: "So you're leaving to paint full-time? Good luck."

At that, a wee wummin in the shop stopped him and asked: "Ah couldnae help overhearin', son. How much dae ye take fur ceilings?"

DO WE believe the chap who tells us that the boss at his factory was irritated by a worker being late back from a fag break outside, and the boss pointed exaggeratedly to an imaginary watch on his arm and shouted: "Hey! What do you call this?"

The smoker merely shouted back: "Your wrist?"

A HUMAN Resources person tells us about the employee, when filling out his personal records file, wrote under "who is to be notified in case of an emergency?" the simple phrase: "An excellent doctor."

A READER tells us he was in the office communal kitchen where he saw a bag with "Spat on" written on the side. He was telling a colleague how disgusting he thought that was but was greeted with a mystified look.

So he pointed again at what was written, until his colleague told him: "That's Sadie Paton's."

JACKIE McFarlane worked in an Uddingston factory where an English supplier calling to chase up an unpaid invoice was helpfully advised that the lady responsible was on a day off, and that he should "call Maggie ramorra". Naturally, the next day the chap phoned and asked: "Can I speak to Miss Ramorra please?"

IT IS 40 YEARS since oil was discovered in the North Sea. Gordon Bickerton tells us about a rescue simulation on a platform where a dummy was thrown overboard for the standby boat to practise a rescue. Unfortunately, a colleague came on deck not realising it was a practice, and seeing the dummy whistle past him from the helideck above, ran for the nearest life belt and threw it in. The belt was attached to a wire, though, and ended up dangling uselessly 10 feet above the now drowning dummy.

As everyone around him collapsed in laughter, the would-be rescuer angrily shouted: "You heartless b******s. There's a man in the water!" thus ensuring further laughter from all around him.

SO, DO we believe the reader who claimed he was on a bus and heard the chap in front tell the female with him that he had just got a job in a bowling alley?

"Tenpin?" she asked him. "No, it's a permanent position," he replied.

WE HEAR about the gas serviceman who arrived at a house in West Lothian with his apprentice and while giving a boiler its winter service, the older fellow was joking with his apprentice that despite the age gap he was still fitter than the youngster.

To settle it, he challenged the apprentice to see who could run back to their van faster.

When they did so they were surprised to see the householder running after them. When they asked him why, he told them: "When I see two gas men running as hard as you two were, I thought I'd better run, too."

GARY Johnston recalls a job-seeking mate telling him that a good interview technique is to imagine the interview panel naked, as it reminds you that they are mere mortals and therefore not to be found intimidating. Unfortunately, his mate was so nervous that he blurted this out at the start of an interview.

Says Gary: "He was rewarded with an excruciating pause and a subsequent half-hour of tortured frostiness from two douce spinsters and a fat middle-aged bloke who were interviewing him. Guess what? He didn't get the job."

BILL Moore told us: "I knew a Glasgow guy who was being interviewed for a general handyman job at McGill University in Montreal. He desperately wanted the job, and the last question in the interview was, 'Tell us, Mr Gallagher, can you do cement work?'

"'Can Ah dae cement work?', he replied. 'Did they find Jimmy Hoffa?'

"Adds Bill: "He's still working at McGill, 20 years later."

AND we don't know what it is about Canada, but reader Anne Baxter tells us her cousin in Canada was interviewing a prospective employee who appeared pretty laid-back.

This was confirmed during the interview when her cousin's PA entered the interview room and said that a pizza delivery chap had arrived.

At that point the laid-back chap stirred himself, and said it was for him. Strangely, he didn't get the job.

A MUM in Glasgow's Garrowhill wanted the spare room turned into a nursery, so she hired a jobbing painter her dad knew. Going in to the nursery to see his work, she was aghast to find that the alphabet border at head level around the room went from A, B, C, up to F, then jumped to P, Q, R.

When she angrily asked the decorator what he had done that for, he defended himself by arguing: "What's the matter wi' ye? The wean cannae read!"

READER Robert Spence, reading *The Herald* story about former crew cleaning the Royal Yacht Britannia, recalls meeting a mate, a diehard communist, for a pint when his friend worked in a shipyard where the Britannia was in for a refit.

"How's life?" asked Robert. "Great!" replied his pal. "I peed in the Queen's sink."

ANDY Collins in North Carolina recalls, as a police officer, directing traffic in Port Glasgow as the yards came out. Suddenly one chap tripped and fell, and lay there like a stricken insect, hands and legs flaying, as he tried in vain to get to his feet.

Andy went over to help and, surprised that he couldn't get the chap back up, then discovered that underneath his coat he was cocooned in yards of welding cable around his body that he had been nicking for scrap.

A READER tells us about a former chief executive of North Ayrshire Council who was known as the Pawnbroker – his standard answer was "leave it with me".

"AT ALBION Motors," says Ian Maclean of Bishopton, "the charge-hand millwright was known as The Abbot. During a discussion he would inevitably chime in with 'Ah, but.'"

JOHN Park in Motherwell tells us about a chap in the factory where he worked who was known as Hip-Hip. His actual name was Hugh Rae.

READER Gordon Martin tells us: "I remember my father talking about a foreman at Babcocks who was known as The Sheriff as he was often heard asking, 'Where's the hold up?'"

THANKS to readers who had a friend named Jim Hughes. We suspect there may have been one or two of them. Those who know the Glasgow vernacular will realise why anyone named Jim Hughes was nicknamed Gutties.

JOE Hunter tells us: "A foreman in the shipyards was known as The Balloon as he was forever telling the workers, 'Don't let me down.'"

WE END workplace nicknames with May Harris telling us: "My husband remembers a well-respected inspection foreman at Rolls-Royce, East Kilbride, in the 1970s, who was affectionately known as Rembrandt. His usual reply to any query or expression of doubt was: 'Let me put you in the picture.'"

22
Taking Your Teeth Out

Every Scotsman loves his mother – but that wouldn't stop him telling a joke about her.

A CHAP in Milngavie phoned his widowed mum to see how she was, not knowing she had bought some flower bulbs at the supermarket that day which she wanted to plant on her husband's grave.

So you can imagine his shock when she told him: "Bring a spade when you come at the weekend. We're going to visit your dad."

A WEST end reader tells us that whenever he is driving his mum home, and he lets another car out from a side road or gives another driver the right of way, he naturally exchanges a wave with the other driver.

"Who's that?" his mother always asks.

A CHAP who took early retirement was regaling his working pals with how great his life now was, and we overhear him end his glowing report with: "Honestly, I've enough money to last me the rest of my life," then added: "Provided I'm dead by a week on Friday."

A READER was giving his ageing mum a lift home when they passed a row of cellophaned bunches of flowers at the side of the road.

"They'll never sell them there – it's a bad corner for folk to stop," she announced.

A STUDENT tells us she took out her laptop when she was visiting her gran in Carntyne – probably trying to check her Facebook messages for the twentieth time that day.

Gran grabbed it, gave it a vigorous shake, and told the student her mother had one when she was small.

Eventually the student worked out that gran thought it was an Etch-a-Sketch.

A READER realised that his elderly mother had left her watch at his home after visiting for the weekend. When he phoned to tell her that he would try to return it to her as soon as possible, she told him: "No great hurry – if I need tae know the time, I'll phone you."

WE OVERHEAR an elderly gent walking down Glasgow's Sauchiehall Street who, after scanning the crowds around him, told his companion:

"In my day, if you wanted to see a fat lady or a tattooed man, you had to go to the circus."

A READER took her aged mum with her when she was looking for a new car the other day, and was doing a tour of the showrooms to see what bargains there were in these recessionary times.

Alas, she just couldn't find what she wanted, and driving home, a little dispirited, she was interrupted by her mum beside her pointing out the window and telling her: "Look at that showroom. If you don't find a car in there, you never will! There are loads of cars."

"That's Morrisons' car park," she had to explain to mum.

AN AYR reader tells us about his elderly mother complaining that she kept missing parts of her television programmes when she went to put the kettle on or went to the toilet.

"You can get one of these digital boxes," he told her. "That freezes the programme while you are out of the room."

"Naw, son, I couldn't do that," she told him. "It wouldn't be fair to all the other folk who were watching it."

A GRANNY was telling her family: "It's changed days these days. I remember you could go to the shops with less than a pound and still be able to come back with a dozen eggs, a chicken, sausages and a tin of custard."

"That's inflation for you," her son piped up.

"Inflation nothing," replied granny. "It's all these security cameras they have in the shops these days."

A CHAP in Mosspark tells us that he was trying to convince his ageing mother that a £900 hearing aid from a private company would be far better for her than the less helpful piece of equipment she had from the NHS, but she was having none of it. "I've never heard a conversation yet," she told him, "that was worth £900."

A MILNGAVIE reader was telling his teenage grand-daughter that the modern generation lacked modesty. "When I was your age," he told her, "girls still knew how to blush."

"For goodness sake, grand-dad," she asked him. "What on earth did you say to them?"

A YOUNG woman dodging through the rain showers in Glasgow's city centre was approached by an old dear who asked her if she by any chance recalled the date of the Battle of Bannockburn.

Not knowing whether this was some sales scam, or even some prize draw, the young woman surprised herself by dragging out from her memory: "1314."

The pensioner politely thanked her, and turned to the cash machine behind her, and tapped in her pin number.

"MY GRAN'S one of those people who thinks a cup of tea is the answer to everything," said the loudmouth in the bar the other night.

"Which is why she was such a disaster when we put her in our pub quiz team."

A READER tells us he was concerned about his ageing mum keeping a wad of banknotes in the top drawer of the bureau in the living room, which could be immediately spotted by any housebreaker.

As she refused to put the cash in the bank, he brought her instead a fake tin of beans which had a bottom which could be removed for hiding cash inside, and would not attract attention in the kitchen cupboard.

He was delighted on his next visit when she confirmed that she was using it – until he opened the bureau drawer in the living room, and there was the fake beans tin.

THE FAMILY of a retired Ayrshire miner, to mark his 90th birthday, applied to the Ministry of Defence for the medals he was due for serving in the Home Guard in Cumnock during the war.

The MoD was interested in the claim that he had been wounded while serving, until told by the family the circumstances that on the first parade night in which they had actual rifles rather than pickaxe handles, he was accidentally shot in the knee by a comrade.

The MoD explained that as this came under the category of "friendly fire" there would be no citation – even when the family wrote back to tell them: "When a man from New Cumnock is wounded, however accidently, by a man from Cumnock, there is no way this can be described as 'Friendly Fire.'"

THE AULD fella in the golf club bar the other day was telling his playing pals: "These days I spend a lot of time thinking about the hereafter."

When they asked him why, he added: "I go into a room in the house, and then think, 'What am I hereafter?'"

FORMER Hutchie Grammar deputy rector, Sandy Strang, now an after-dinner speaker, told of the heartache of putting an uncle into a nursing home when he couldn't cope living on his own.

Sandy phoned the home the next day to find out how he was faring, and the matron told Sandy his uncle was like a fish out of water.

"Is he not settling in?" asked Sandy. "No," explained matron. "He's deid."

AN EXPATRIATE home from Cape Town was in a Dumfries post office when an elderly man at the front of the queue was being taken through some security questions in order to access his account. He was asked for his mother's maiden name. He said it was Mary. The man behind the counter explained that was her Christian name, not her maiden name.

As he stood there, looking blank, an exasperated voice shouted from the back of the queue: "Mary whit?"

23
Sell By Date

A SIGN of the times, as primary teacher Rosemary Sanders in Ellon, Aberdeenshire, tells us she finished a discussion on the Battle of Bannockburn by saying that the class could visit the site of the battle.

A hand went up and a young lad asked if the site was www. bannockburn.com.

WE HEAR about a heated primary school football game where the referee calls an eight-year-old over and says: "Do you know you shouldn't call the referee a complete waste of space who has lost his guide dog?"

"Yes," says the little boy. "And you know you shouldn't call the opposition defence a bunch of cheating divers."

"Yes," he says.

"Good," adds the ref. "Now go over to your shouting mother and explain it to her."

A NURSE delivering a sex education lesson to a class of first-year pupils in Glasgow was treated with world-weary cynicism when she asked if they all knew what a condom was. Sadly, it was only when she said she was going to put it on a courgette did the class sit up and ask, "What's that?" in baffled astonishment.

SO ARE there differences between kids from posh schools and those from the state sector? We only ask after a matinee performance, packed with school pupils, of the RSAMD's Christmas panto in Glasgow, Jack and the Beanstalk, when the baddie Ab Fab was looking for the hapless Marble Archie. When he asked where he was, most kids were shouting with gusto the timeless line: "He's behind you," while a row of feepaying pupils from St Aloysius were sitting putting their hands up to answer.

A PRIMARY teacher tells us she asked her class, on a lesson on stranger danger, why they should not accept sweets from a stranger.

"They might be past their sell-by date," piped up one little youngster.

WE HEAR from a primary school where a student teacher in her first placement is in charge of the class which has just had a visitor who had brought along his dog.

The dog owner said it was OK to clap the dog, so the student teacher encouraged the children to give it a big round of applause.

AT AN east end Glasgow primary school, a firefighter in uniform was invited along from the local station to give a safety talk to pupils about the dangers of fire.

Summing up what he had told the kids about safety around the home, he asked the class: "And why do you not touch a cooker or toaster?"

First pupil with his hand up replied: "Fingerprints."

A SCIENCE teacher said he couldn't wait for his holidays when he told his class to have one beaker of boiled water and the other with unboiled water in front of them for the next experiment.

"Please, sir," asked a pupil. "How do you unboil water?"

24
Shopping Around

A READER was in a garden centre where he watched a fellow customer pick up a packet of insecticide and ask: "Is this good for greenfly?"

"No," said the cheery salesperson, "it'll kill them."

THE GARDEN centre story reminded Bert Peattie in Kirkcaldy of a pal of his, highly qualified in horticulture, who was approached by a chap who asked him: "Ah've goat greenfly oan ma roses. Is it right that ye jist have tae spray them wi' soapy watter?"

"Aye," replied Bert's worthy mate, "providing yer only wantin' tae nip their een."

AN ASSISTANT in a tile shop tells us a potential customer phoned and asked how much it would cost to have her bathroom laid. "Depends on the area," the assistant told her.

"Carntyne," the woman replied. "But why would that affect the price?"

WE HAVE lightly made fun of bookshop assistants misunderstanding inquiries, so we should pass on a story from one such assistant who said a chap came in and asked if they stocked any plays by Shakespeare.

"Which one?" the assistant asked.

"William," the customer replied.

A READER in a Glasgow supermarket, heard a young girl say to her mum: "Can we get some strawberries?"

But her mum replied: "No. We got them last week and they were totally tasteless. Just like eating water."

But her daughter persisted: "It's two packets for the price of one."

"OK then," said her mum.

A READER was chatting to a friend in Edinburgh who is a music teacher. She decided to jazz up the certificates she presented to pupils by using sealing wax to make them look more imposing, but wondered if shops still sold it. She realised how difficult a task it was after phoning a number of stores to no avail, until one assistant asked her: "I've never heard of anyone polishing their ceilings. Would floor wax not do?"

SOMEONE unlikely to get a treat one day was the little lad being dragged out shopping in Glasgow with his mum who had to wait while she tried on a pair of fashionably-ripped jeans. She looked not best pleased when he piped up: "Mum, people will see your hairy legs."

WE FEARED the worst when a chap out shopping with his girlfriend last weekend, and clearly bored with the whole process, was inevitably asked when she popped out of the changing room: "Do these trousers make my bum look big."

Clearly the bravery pills had kicked in as he couldn't stop himself from replying: "No, I think it's pies that do that."

READER Rob Mackenzie tells us of a store customer who complained: "I've been ringing your 0800 freephone number and getting no reply."

"I didn't know we had a freephone number. Where did you get it from?" asked the assistant.

"Outside on your door," said the customer. "0800 1730."

"That's our opening hours," replied the assistant.

A CHAP working in a Glasgow gents' outfitters tells us about the woman who came in last week seeking a dress shirt for her husband. When he asked for the collar size, her face fell until she finally told him: "I know this sounds daft, but when I make a circle with my thumbs and first fingers, it fits perfectly around his neck."

A PART-TIME worker in Boots tells us about a customer leaving his mobile phone on the counter. So she scrolled through the saved numbers, stopped at "Mum" and phoned the woman to tell her that her son had left his phone in the shop.

"Don't worry," said the mum, "I'll take care of it."

Two minutes later, the mobile rang and the assistant couldn't stop herself from answering, to hear a woman's voice: "Martin. You've gone and left your phone in Boots."

NEWS that the charming Edinburgh lingerie shop Boudiche opened a branch in Glasgow's Ingram Street reminds us of the customer who asked: "I'd like a pair of stockings for my wife."

"Sheer?" asked the assistant. "No, she's at home," he replied.

"STORE staff are getting ruder," opined the chap in the pub the other night.

"I was in my local record store and asked if they had anything by The Doors.

"The guy behind the counter said, 'Sure. A fat security guard and a *Big Issue* seller.'"

A GLAMOROUS thirtysomething woman trying on a black suit in a Glasgow store the other week was approached by a fellow shopper, as happens in Glasgow, and was told that she looked fabulous in the outfit.

"Is it for a special occasion?" the chatty woman asked.

"Yes," the woman in the suit replied. "My husband's funeral."

"Oh, I'm terribly sorry," the inquisitive one asked. "When is it?"

"I don't know," said the woman in the suit. "I haven't killed him yet."

THE IMPENDING onslaught of Christmas shopping reminds us of the harassed woman wrapping a late Christmas present for one of her daughter's friends, when her little girl pointed out as she finished that the wrapping paper was printed with "Happy Birthday".

"Just write Jesus below it," said her exasperated mum.

A READER tells us he bought some dodgy tat at the Barras, but had been reassured by the sign on the vendor's pitch stating: "Money back if not completely satisfied."

Unfortunately, what he bought didn't work, so he took it back and asked for a refund, but was refused.

So he pointed at the sign and was told: "It's OK. We were completely satisfied with your money."

TOM Law in Hunter's Quay was chatting to a shop owner who told him that a customer brought back a telephone she had been given as a present, claiming that it wasn't working properly.

The shop owner unplugged the shop phone, stuck the woman's phone in the socket instead, and dialled the shop's number on his mobile phone.

As the woman's phone began ringing she stared at it in amazement and asked the chap: "But how did you know my number?"

A TEENAGE boy out shopping with his dad in Glasgow's city centre in the Christmas Eve buying frenzy, and clearly unable to find a present for his dad's mum, was heard telling him: "Wasn't it easier when you could stick a piece of macaroni on a bit of cardboard and say, 'Here, Gran, I made this for you?' "

WE ARE told about the woman in the Clydebank supermarket who put her few items on the conveyor belt and, frustrated that the check-out assistant had his back to her while chatting to a work colleague, eventually shouted: "Excuse me. Can I get checked out?"

The young chap turned round, looked her up and down, and announced: "No' bad."

PAISLEY reader Robert McMillan was in his local Tesco admiring a display of food for Burns Night, which had a very large haggis, tatties, neeps, Burns country cheese, and Belhaven Robert Burns Ale. The shopper next to him seemed less impressed as he declared: "Nae wonder he died at 37, eatin' aw that rubbish."

25
Our Lovely Politicians

GORDON Brown was reminiscing at the opening of the new BBC headquarters in Glasgow about his early days at rivals Scottish Television when he had to handle phone complaints from the public.

He said his boss advised him: "Be very courteous, and start by asking the number of their TV licence."

Magically, many callers then hung up.

AN OVERUSED phrase by unfortunates on *Tricia*, *Big Brother* or the *Jeremy Kyle Show* is "24/7", the American phrase for all the time.

Western Isles councillor Norman Macleod, clearly aware of the religious sensibilities of his background, took office as convener of the Northern Police Board and pledged he would have "an open-door policy – 24/6".

GERRY MacKenzie heard a chap in the pub announce: "I was reading that American President Barack Obama is claiming Scottish blood in his ancestry."

"Would that be the Maryhill Baracks?" replied his drinking buddy.

"I WENT to buy a car," said the chap in the pub the other night, "and the salesman offered the option of HP or MP."

"When I asked him what MP was," added the toper, "he said I got the car, but some other mug paid for it."

"MY LOCAL corner shop has changed the notice in its window," said the chap in the bar the other night. "It now reads, 'Only one MP allowed in the shop at any time.'"

THE EXPENSES debacle reminds us of when former Tory minister Jonathan Aitken went to jail for perjury.

The story at the time was that when he was leaving the nick at the end of his sentence, a fellow lag asked him: "Are you going to go straight – or are you going back into politics?"

"I NO LONGER want to become an MP," said the chap in the pub the other night.

"I mean, if you can't get your moat cleaned on expenses, what's the point?" he added.